AWAK

This book gives a much-needed wake-up call for Christians in the arts. Tyler encourages creatives to embrace their God-given talents and create art that makes a difference. As a film producer with a successful Christian tv series, I'd recommend this book to anyone who is looking to pursue excellence with the Lord in their creativity.

CHAD GUNDERSEN

Film & TV Producer | *The Chosen*

I pray that all of us, no matter where we are on the spectrum of "artist", take this message to heart. If creating is important to God, it should be important to us. We are all artists in some form, made in the image of God. This book is an incredibly powerful reminder of that.

DUSTIN TAVELLA

Magician & Singer | *America's Got Talent*: 2021 Winner

A thought provoking template for anyone with a creative "itch". This book has a unique way of translating the industry structure while also being "thought conscious" and morally grounded. In a world primarily known for introducing "NEW" ideas, I personally enjoy the way Tyler empowers creativity from and through the Holy Spirit.

MATTHEW SMITH

Actor & Model | *New Girl & America's Next Top Model*

As a producer and studio owner that has worked with Tyler, this book is a perfect example of how he lives out his daily journey with the Holy Spirit. Tyler articulates how to partner with the Holy Spirit in so many new and innovative ways that will awaken fresh dreams and visions in your life. This is a timely message every creative needs to consume.

AMBER BUTAUD
Producer & Studio Owner | 4 The One Studio

Brent + Molly

Love Y'all!

Tyler C

TYLER W. CHILDS

AWAKEN O DREAMER

your creativity awaits...

ISBN: 979-8-9879730-0-4

Library of Congress Control Number: 2023904666

Front cover design by Janis Oppliger | Wave Crusher Studio
Book design by Allan Nygren | Mosaic Productions
Hand Lettering by Nelson Carreño | Neto
Development edit by Kai Elwyn
Copy edit by Kristen Defevers

Printed in the United States of America.

First printing edition 2023.

Parable International
5900 Balcones Drive, STE 100
Austin, TX, 78731
www.parableint.org

Acknowledgments

This book would be nothing today without the Lord and his guidance. God is so good and I am incredibly honored to have been a vessel for this project.

To the love of my life, Becca, you are the most amazing woman I've ever met. Thank you for challenging me to always pursue God's plans for our lives and take risks.

To my three little dreamers: Riverlyn, Zion & Eden. You are my pride and joy! Never stop listening to the Lord's voice and sharing his love with those around you.

To our friends and family: Thank you for putting up with me and my crazy ideas. Your support throughout the years and constant encouragement mean the world to me.

I love all of you and am so blessed to have you in my life! You are seen and have impacted me in more ways than I can count!

Table of Contents

Foreword

What if I told you that within the pages of this book is a secret knowledge, the source of unmatched, limitless creativity? This knowledge is the same knowledge that has been the source of inspiration for the greatest artists and thinkers throughout history. Sounds too good to be true, right?

As the Creative Director at the nation's "fastest growing" megachurch, there was great demand on me and my team to continually produce ever better, cutting edge, and more engaging productions. Our organization placed a high value on immersive experiences for our congregation. My team was often referred to as the Imagineers of the Church world.

I had worked in the creative industry for twenty-plus years and fresh ideas didn't come as easily as they once did. Planning 53 unique church services a year is like feeding a beast that consumes any good (and bad) ideas you ever had. Even still, we committed to taking our productions to even new creative heights; so I began looking for a new, out-of-the-box creative thinker to bring fresh ideas to the team. After an exhaustive nationwide search, God led us to Tyler.

Tyler brought with him a respectable acumen and a long list of achievements from the creative and film worlds: Producer at National Geographic, award-winning film Director and Producer, and content creator for the Bevere's at Messenger International, just to name a few. He brought with him many qualities, but I was most excited about his views on being Spirit lead and walking with God. His spiritual maturity was a welcome addition to our overburdened team.

Tyler had committed much of his life to spiritual development. He spent years with organizations like YWAM, studied at Christian schools, and worked as a youth pastor leading teenagers into deeper relationships with their faith. As Tyler grew in his faith, he became attuned to seeking God's face, hearing God's voice, and then following God's calling.

I remember vividly the first brainstorming meeting where Tyler was present. We were tasked to make a film for our upcoming Easter services and we met to generate some initial theme ideas. I began the meeting as usual, I pulled out my dry-erase marker and began writing some ideas onto the whiteboard. The team looked at me blank-faced. What did I expect, the ideas were derivative and were missing that spark of inspiration. Where would the next great idea come from?

I looked to the new guy, "whatcha got Tyler?". Experience had taught me the immense value of the "outsiders perspective" and in this case, Tyler did not disappoint. "Well, have you guys tried inviting the Holy Spirit into your creative process?" Tyler suggested. Who did this guy think he was? I thought to myself, "We were the church experts, of course, we had… Had we?" We frequently opened our meetings with a quick prayer, but we never even considered inviting the Spirit directly into the process. To be honest, it seemed a little weird, but my interest had been piqued. "Go on, what is it that you mean exactly?"

Tyler suggested that we start by praying and then invite The Holy Spirit to join us in the room. To ask for His partnership and His favor in our brainstorming meeting. To earnestly seek His will to be done, not our own, and that our own voices would be silent so that we could hear His voice. I begrudgingly agreed to the exercise. We prayed and then we all just sat there in silence for 30 minutes, just listening for direction from the Spirit. It felt like an eternity.

What came out of that time of quiet listening was nothing short of astonishing. Each of us had heard something special from God. We wrote those ideas down, discussed them, and built our film script around them. That simple act of faith kicked off an astonishing journey in the making of that film. A seed was planted by the Spirit that day and we asked God to walk alongside us every step of the way. We witnessed miracles happen, cast and crew members come to faith, healings, and eventually thousands of lives were impacted by our film. To our astonishment, the film went on to win accolades and laurels at major international film festivals. All we could say was "to God be the glory!" and we meant it. And most importantly the spiritual discipline of inviting the Holy Spirit into our process became part of our normal workflow and it elevated our work for years to come.

So to answer my question to you, yes, unequivocally, "within the pages of this book lies a secret knowledge and the source of unparalleled, limitless creativity". The knowledge that Tyler, the author of this book, has aggregated for you is the transcendent understanding that has inspired countless creatives over the millennia and I now count myself among them.

In our subsequent years of collaboration, there have been many other invaluable lessons that I have learned from Tyler and his inspired approach to creativity. Many of those stories you will find here, within the pages of this book. But I would be remiss if I didn't tell you at least one more quick story about Tyler and his wife Becca.

In the spring of 2020, the fallout from the Covid-19 lockdowns devastated our church and along with it our creative department. After all, a church with shuttered doors is no church at all. At that time we witnessed what we thought was the end of our livelihoods as Covid layoffs shattered our team and our lives. Overnight we were fractured and scattered, but through that process I witnessed Tyler and Becca lean into their faith rather than run from it.

> 'Jesus answered, "If you want to be perfect, go, sell your possessions and give to the poor, and you will have treasure in heaven. Then come, follow me."'
>
> - Matthew 19:21

After months of prayer and listening to the Spirit, Tyler, and Becca doubled down on their faith and risked it all to follow Jesus. They sold their house and all of their worldly possessions, loaded their 3 small children into an RV, and hit the road; free to share with others what they've learned about Jesus and their spiritual disciplines. They started their ministry, Parable International, and began traveling the U.S. and the world, teaching ministries about creativity and storytelling within God's favor.

In the subsequent years I've witnessed Tyler and Becca spread their message from the U.S. to the Czech Republic, to poverty-stricken parts of Brazil and Mexico, and to the war-stricken people of Ukraine. Tyler and Becca truly live out what Tyler shares in this book. It is their way of life.

Looking back I suppose I was a guinea pig of sorts, an unwitting subject on which Tyler could refine these teachings. I pray that you'll open your hearts and minds to its content and like me, through this process, you will find great meaning and purpose in your creative endeavors.

Ryan C. Chapel
Creative Director & Filmmaker

INTRODUCTION

Hey there, thanks so much for taking the time to explore fresh creativity with the Lord. I pray that as you read this book, new dreams, and visions will be poured out and you'll be encouraged to pursue them with the childlike faith we once knew. This book is a piece of something the Lord is doing with our ministry, Parable International. I truly believe there is a new creative awakening coming and that by reading this book, you are saying *yes* to what the Lord has in store for you. New things are coming, friends. God is working and moving. Be prepared to witness and take part in creative excellence, unlike anything we've ever seen before. This isn't limited to just films (although I'm biased as a filmmaker); we are going to see, hear, and experience art that will change the world.

You may be wondering what to expect with a book like this. My intention is to walk you through a process that will allow you to open your heart to something different and experience God—possibly in ways you haven't before. We are going to discuss what it means to be someone who relies on the Holy Spirit for inspiration and direction. I hope that by the time you set

xvi   Awaken O Dreamer

this book down, you'll have a dream from God burning in your heart. I'm going to place you into the slingshot, pull it back, and prepare you for launch, but at the end of the day, it will be up to you to let go of what is comfortable and pull that lever.

This book is here to support your dreams and visions. There is no qualification needed to consume this material. My prayer is that doctors, engineers, accountants, carpenters, moms, dads, husbands, wives, and anyone with breath in their lungs find a new part of themselves in this book. You have dreams and ideas for a reason; they aren't in your heart by accident. So here's to you, taking the first step toward waking up to something new. It's time to awaken, O Dreamer.

Let's pray:

> Lord, I ask that every person reading this book would tangibly encounter you. I ask that you would give them ears to hear you and a receptive heart. We know that James 1:17 says, "Every good and every perfect gift is from above, coming down from the Father of lights." We say yes to this, Lord. You are the great inspirer, the Creator of creativity, the One who gives and takes away. God, you are good. We trust you, and we invite you into this process; we invite you to speak to us. We love you, Father. Help us be more like you every day. Protect us; guard our hearts and our ideas from our flesh and anything else that would seek to tarnish your name.

We submit all these things to you and thank you for your willingness to partner with us. In the mighty name of Jesus, Amen.

.

1

You Can Hear the Voice of God, Bro?

Can I be honest with you? Writing a book has been intimidating for me. It's taken a lot of discipline for me to just sit, pray, and write, but I know it's worth it. This book is going to strategically build on itself and hopefully you'll walk away with more than just encouragement. However, before we move forward in this book, we need to set a precedent and talk through a fundamental part of our walk with Jesus.

Do you know that Jesus speaks to you?

Depending on your background, you may have grown up in a church that believed that or one that didn't; or maybe you didn't grow up in the church. Regardless of your faith background, it's essential that we establish how Jesus communicates with each one of us. By the time you move on from this chapter, you will hopefully have a new understanding of how the Lord can speak to us and tools to help you actively listen.

For years, this has been a favorite topic of mine to teach on. Sometimes churches reach out to me and ask, "Can you teach anything non-film related?" Hearing the voice of God is always my first suggestion. The subject gets me so excited because it's such a pivotal part of your walk with Jesus to explore.

Once I was a producer on a Western movie. This was a secular project, but a handful of the key crew were Christians. While I wasn't preaching on set or anything, I kept my head down and did my best to make sure the crew was being treated well and valued. I'll never forget the moment when the costume gal approached me with some surprising comments. She mentioned that she had Facebook stalked me and discovered that in addition to making films, I also run a ministry. She said that it had piqued her interest, so she stumbled upon our ministry page and even ended up watching a message I had preached in a church about hearing the voice of God. Mind you, this was all said in front of one of our actors.

Now, this conversation could have gone one of two ways, and I didn't know what her reaction would be. She looked at me after saying all that and thanked me, because she could hear the voice of the Lord now. I was floored. First, because I wasn't expecting to have this type of conversation on a secular movie set. Second, because she was so bold in her faith that she didn't care if our actor overheard her newfound discovery. I stood there for a second in shock and looked over at our wide-eyed actor. Then he said, "You can hear the voice of God, bro?" When I confirmed that I could, he started opening up to us about his struggles to find God and his desire for prayer. That is a day that will forever be marked on my heart; I learned that my time on set would never be the same.

You can hear the voice of God, bro! Let's learn how.

In the Bible, there are two specific ways that God speaks to his people. The two Greek words we often see in the text are *logos* and *rhema*, and both can be translated as "word" or "sayings." It's not until we dive into the context and the deeper meaning that we truly discover the Lord's intent for each word. The first, *logos*, is often used to refer to the written Word, such as the Bible or the gospel; some translations even use words like "principle" or "reason." Here are some examples found in Scripture.

Matthew 7:24: "Everyone therefore who hears these words [*logos*] of mine and does them, I will liken him to a wise man who built his house on a rock."

Luke 5:1: "Now while the multitude pressed on him and heard the word [*logos*] of God, he was standing by the lake of Gennesaret."

Acts 6:7a: "The word [*logos*] of God increased and the number of the disciples greatly multiplied in Jerusalem."

These verses hopefully give you good context. There are countless resources out there that allow you to dig deeper if you really want to learn more about the Greek translation of *logos*. For our purposes, we just need to know that *logos* is often referred to as the written Word of God. This is essential to our faith. We, as Christians, hold the Bible as the infallible and unchanging Word of God.

The second word is *rhema*, and it's just as important as *logos*. *Rhema* is the spoken and inspired word of God. *Logos* gives us something to live by, *rhema* gives us something to live with. It's the breath of life in the Scriptures, the "holy nudge," as the Newsboys called it. A quick example of *rhema* can be found in Romans 10:17, which says, "So faith comes by hearing, and hearing by the word [*rhema*] of God." Oftentimes, *rhema* is what allows us to interpret the Scriptures, and it's how the Lord can speak to you directly out of the written text.

Let's take this a step further: *rhema* is how the Holy Spirit speaks to us. It's the still, small voice that guides, convicts, encourages, and more. I know most of you probably know who the Holy Spirit is, but I want to take a second to paint a picture for you. Do you remember the 1940s animated film *Pinocchio*? A few years back, the Lord pointed out a moment in that movie to me that is a brilliant example of the Holy Spirit's role in our life. Early on in the movie, Jiminy Cricket asks the Fairy if he can be Pinocchio's conscience and is then described as "the still, small voice… Lord High Keeper of the knowledge of right and wrong, counselor in moments of temptation, and guide along the straight and narrow path." Can we just take a pause for a minute and acknowledge this… Disney just described the Holy Spirit. I've used this analogy for years with youth students and others alike; it's the perfect visual for the third member of the Holy Trinity.

John 15:26 says, "When the Counselor has come, whom I will send to you from the Father, the Spirit of truth, who proceeds from the Father, he will testify about me."

The Holy Spirit has come to testify of the Lord because he's the Spirit of truth and life. The Holy Spirit was Jesus' parting gift to Christians as he ascended into heaven. He gave us direct access to the Father through the Spirit that lives in us. The Holy Spirit exists to speak life into us, convict us, and guide us daily. You may be sitting there wondering about this Holy Spirit, asking, "Does he truly live in me?" Well, let me ask you this… Have

MY SHEEP HEAR
MY VOICE
I KNOW THEM
and

JOHN 10:27

you ever felt a conviction about something? The answer is probably yes. Sometimes, we do something called quenching the Holy Spirit. It happens when we ignore that still, small voice or conviction; we choose what we want, regardless of the consequences. Over time, we become callous to the Holy Spirit and forget what it was like to hear his voice or feel his comfort. It's not something to feel ashamed of—we've all done it. Most folks, including myself, have gone through seasons where we choose worldly pleasures; we try our best to ignore the Lord and keep him in the walls of the church. If that's you right now, I want you to know that it's not too late. He still loves you and cares for you. If you're willing to walk away from those things separating you from him, he's standing there with open arms.

This reminds me of the story of the prodigal son (Luke 15:11-32). The younger son takes his inheritance and follows his flesh, but in the end, it just leads to emptiness and misery. He chooses to return home, and even when he's still a long way off, his father sees him and begins running to him, exclaiming loudly that his child has returned at last. The same is true with you: no matter how far you've run or how many other things you've used to distract you, your Heavenly Father sits waiting to talk to you. He cares that much about you; he loves you more than you know and is eager to have conversations with his children.

What does it look like to talk to God? Well, I think there's a better question to ask: What does it look like to listen to God? We all do a lot of talking, especially in times of need. "God, help me with this meeting, this test, this relationship"—and the list goes on and on. All those things are fine and dandy, but we need to ask for more than just a leg up. It's important to ask him for direction and for his thoughts on your current situation. Your prayer times will become more and more fruitful the more you learn to be still and listen.

This chapter is important because we are going to explore what it means to truly hear his voice. John 10:27 says, "My sheep hear my voice, and I know them, and they follow me." The reason sheep listen to their shepherd's voice is because they recognize him; they know that he's their protector. This reminds me of a viral video I saw once. The video begins with a shepherd showing a group of folks his sheep; he tells different individuals to try and call the sheep. One by one, each spectator tries to get the attention of the herd. They holler and offer treats, but to no avail: the sheep won't even look up from their mindless grazing. Then the shepherd calls them. Sure enough, it only takes one word from a familiar voice and, in an instant, all the sheep come running. This video shows us how valuable it is to recognize his voice.

In our quiet times, there are four different voices we can hear, and it's up to us to recognize the Father's voice. I'm going to list all four and provide you with some keys to help prepare your heart to listen and determine what voice is the voice of truth.

Voice 1: Our Own Voice
This is the hardest voice to separate from the voice of God. When we begin praying, our selfish nature may try to derail or manipulate what the Lord is saying. We've got to set aside our desires, die to our own imaginations, and submit ourselves to him wholly.

Voice 2: The Voices of Others
It's really easy to get into prayer and begin hearing someone else's voice or opinion. Our prayer time can be influenced by family, leaders, teachers, friends, and so many others. Remember, this

is your one-on-one time with God. Those people may have something beneficial to say (or not), but their speech needs to be confirmed by the Lord through his spoken or written word.

Voice 3: The Voice of the Enemy

Satan is a liar. He does what he can to make you feel like garbage, change you, and manipulate what you're hearing. Take a stand against him and the spirits that come with him; fear, lust, selfishness, jealousy, and the rest do not have the right to speak to you.

Voice 4: The Voice of God

At last, the voice you *should* be listening to. This still, small voice will always encourage you and speak life to you. He may bring conviction, but he will never bring condemnation. His words bring comfort and peace.

These four voices can seem either overwhelming or elementary depending on the way you think and how you view your relationship with God. I urge you to think about the differences between them as you sit in silence, listening. Don't worry, this isn't where I leave you just yet. I've presented the four voices you might hear. Now, how do we separate them?

Several years ago, I met an amazing woman named Donna Jordan. Mama Donna, as she's known by me and so many others, teaches on hearing the voice of God with Youth with a Mission (YWAM). She was the first person I'd ever met who was able to articulate so beautifully what it means to hear the voice of God. When I was 18 years old, I attended a discipleship training school with YWAM in Kona, Hawaii… tough location, I know. While teaching, she presented a challenge to our class. She mentioned that everyone struggles to distinguish the voice of God sometimes, but practice makes perfect. The more we practice, the more his voice becomes recognizable and undeniable amid this loud world. To become like a child who knows their father's voice and doesn't doubt it for a second, we would need to train our hearts and ears to listen. She wanted us to reach a place where when we heard God's voice, we would go, "Yeah, that's my dad." You know that you know. So Mama Donna gave us a challenge that I now have taught youth students and folks that want to learn more about the voice of the Father.

Okay, Tyler, what was the challenge?

For the next seven days, when you wake up in the morning, while everything is fresh and new, utter this sentence and listen for a response: "Good morning, Jesus, I love you." To take this challenge seriously, this has to be the *very* first thing you do each morning. Place a reminder on a sticky note on your nightstand or wall or even over your phone screen. Listen for his voice while there is nothing else to distract you and no one else is speaking to you… Who knows, your flesh may still be asleep too, ha! The key is to listen for a response. Some mornings, you may hear, "I love you, too," and some mornings you might hear more! Most folks report that they feel like they can hear a little more day by day. Some people have turned this seven-day challenge into a lifelong routine—that's totally up to you. Think of this as a "wake up with Jesus" moment; it doesn't have to take more than a minute or two. You see, every time you do this, you are training your heart and soul to listen for that specific voice. The repetition will pay off. You've got to continue to practice hearing his voice. Eventually you will have an "aha moment." Just like those sheep who are going about their business, that voice will come in and you will know in an instant, "*That's my dad!*"

Disclaimer: God doesn't operate in any formula or equation, so while this exercise is helpful, I can't guarantee anything. It's helped lots of folks, but an important thing to highlight is that it's meant to help you prepare your heart. This doesn't mean that you will sit down and hear something right off the bat. This takes time and practice just like everything else. He will definitely be speaking to you, but it can take time and repetition to recognize his voice. I believe in you, friend... Don't get frustrated if on the first, second, or even tenth time you feel like you aren't hearing right or are just getting one word. I'm right there with you! There are for sure times that I sit down and feel like I am coming away with just a single word—or even nothing.

I want to encourage you. This chapter has great steps to prepare your heart, and even a fun exercise, but don't ever get discouraged if it's not happening overnight. I urge you to continue to research more about the Holy Spirit. Spend time in the Word, be purposeful about listening to the Lord in your quiet times. Every person is different, and there is nothing wrong with that; just give it time. He *is* speaking, and we just need our hearts to be ready to receive his words. So what are you waiting for? Start practicing, and I'll see you in the next chapter!

REFLECT AND MEDITATE

I encourage you to get alone, somewhere quiet, and seek the Lord's face. Think about everything you've read in this chapter. What is the Lord speaking to you? I've written some questions below and provided a Bible verse to help guide your quiet reflection with the Lord.

Reflect

Do I know my Father's voice?

Am I being intentional in my time with the Lord?

Is there anything hindering me from hearing the voice of God?

How can I better pursue my time with Him?

Meditate

John 10:27-30: "My sheep hear my voice, and I know them, and they follow me. I give eternal life to them. They will never perish, and no one will snatch them out of my hand. My Father who has given them to me is greater than all. No one is able to snatch them out of my Father's hand. I and the Father are one."

Prayer

Lord, help me hear your voice more clearly. I ask that you point out anything that is distracting me from growing closer to you. Help me push my flesh aside and pursue you freely. I lay down my own personal desires and just want the fullness you have for me. Thank you for speaking to me! I surrender my own thoughts to you and ask that you would open my ears to receive all that you have for me. I love you, Lord. Amen.

Use this space to write, sketch and respond to the Lord.

2

Born to Dream

You made it! There are going to be folks that read the first chapter and put the book down who promise to pick it back up but never do; however, you're not one of those people. Every story and dream starts one day at a time. Our pastor used to tell us that the end goal is useless without understanding that it takes daily victories. Let's get started by focusing on each daily victory, writing it down, and celebrating each day you accomplish. As we move forward, continue to write down the things the Lord is speaking to you on this creative journey.

Let's go back to your childhood. Do you remember what it was like to have an imagination? I can't recall the first time I used my imagination, but I sure remember playing make believe with my brother in our backyard. There were days we were pirates or ninjas or maybe even both! It's funny looking back at those memories because our play felt so real. The fictitious narrative we created was our world, complete with danger, adrenaline, humor, and more. I so clearly remember playing war as a kid at the playground and believing so strongly that the enemy was behind every slide and structure. When I think about childhood imagination, I get the biggest grin, and now I get to experience it all over again through the eyes of my children.

Something that still amazes me is that no one has to teach kids how to have imaginations; it just comes naturally. You can go anywhere in the world, and you will always find kids playing with their imaginations. Sometimes they are pretending they are famous soccer players, sometimes warriors or princesses— imagination has no borders. This ability to dream and create with our minds is something the Lord placed in us from the very beginning. I could sit and watch my children make up worlds and places all day long. Imagination is such an amazing tool we were born with, yet culturally, it's not accepted beyond a certain age. We're told that it's time to grow up, face reality, and get a real job. This hurts my heart, friends. There are so many dreamers who could have pursued something more, but they gave up because the world drew a line in the sand. As we grew up, we were influenced by school and those around us to start thinking logically. We were told that dreams don't put food on the table. I am incredibly grateful that my parents continued to encourage me to pursue creativity as I grew up. I don't want to throw anyone under the bus, but unfortunately my parents' creative outlook is not common among parents, teachers, and friends.

It's important not to blame anyone for our unpursued dreams. At the end of the day, they were just repeating something they were told growing up. I say it's time to restore broken dreams; it's never too late. I remember a story I heard on the radio about an older man. He was being interviewed for his one hundredth birthday. The interviewer asked him for any life advice he may have. His response will forever be ingrained in my mind: he said that it is never too late to try something new. He began to talk about how he only started learning to play the piano in his seventies. There were plenty of naysayers who told him he was too old to start something new, yet now he's been playing for thirty years. Folks, we don't know how much time the Lord has us on the earth for, but it's worth pursuing a dream regardless of how late in life you feel you are.

This chapter is meant to inspire you. In case you haven't heard, you have permission to dream, my friend. The Lord sees your heart; he gave you those dreams and visions, so it's time to pursue them. Imagine you are standing in front of an old bookshelf, looking through the dust-covered books, and each title describes a different dream you had. I urge you to begin praying about the possibility of exploring them with the Holy Spirit. He will guide you to the right one, blow off the dust, and say, "It's time." Some of you may not have old dreams, and that's okay. Maybe there are new ones that are just the size of a seed right now. It's time to start praying for these seeds to get watered, germinate, and grow.

I believe there is a new era of dreamers awakening. The Lord is moving about the earth looking for those who will say *yes* to dream with him. While you're reading this book, you could be feeling a tug in your heart. If that's you, oh boy, take his hand and go! This is where fear can come in and try to manipulate the truth, but let me tell you, fear is a liar. Also, when I say to take his hand and go, I'm not saying to drop what you're doing right now; prayer and confirmation is so important.

When the pandemic hit the world in 2020, I lost my job, along with so many other people. I was working at a large church as the Creative Producer. That summer, I applied to over a hundred jobs and got over a hundred denials. I was so discouraged and felt borderline hopeless. I thank God for a wife who is courageous and encouraging; she helped me get through that season with such grace and diligence. I tried to walk away from the creative world. I was burned out, tired, and left feeling insecure about my talents. It was during that time that a friend recommended that we take that time to do a short-term mission trip with YWAM. Full transparency: I laughed. I thought, "Why on earth would I take a family of five on a six-month mission trip?" I made every excuse in the book, including telling my wife, "I'm at the top of my career, why would I walk away from that?" I know, I know, that was a pretty stupid thing to say… Well, I ate those words. My wife so kindly responded by reminding me that currently, I didn't have a career and the film world wasn't even operating in the middle of the pandemic. Defeated and humbled, I agreed to take the trip.

Over a period of six months, my family went to new depths with the Lord and learned to serve the Lord as a family unit. My small children began to hear the voice of God and became little prayer warriors, my wife became an intercessor, and I was called to a new kind of leadership.

After graduation, we heard the Lord so clearly speak the vision of Parable International. God started sharing with us that there are creatives all over the world who are just waiting to be

FOR WE ARE GOD'S MASTERPIECE

EPHESIANS 2:10

activated, trained, and sent. So we began considering what it would look like to launch a creative training school. The more we prayed, the more God revealed to us that this school was a long-term goal, but first we needed to be mobile and accessible. With that, God confirmed with both Becca and I that we needed to sell our house and hit the road full time.

Can we just talk about all the reasons we could have said no? We went from having a four-bedroom house down to a 36-foot travel trailer. We gave up what was comfortable because the Lord asked us to go. I'm not saying this for accolades—this journey was and is still hard in more ways than one, but it is so worth it. I'm telling you this because it would have been so easy to say no to these dreams that my wife and I had. We love to be comfortable, we don't love change, but God thrives in change! I had a vision while praying for confirmation about our trip. I saw myself standing on a river bend, and there was a wooden raft tied up in the rushing water. I could see the point I wanted to reach on the other side of the river, but there was no oar for the raft, not to mention there would be no way to paddle across the river's swift rapids. The Lord told me to get in the boat, but I told him that it would take me downstream and I'd miss the dock on the other side. He kindly questioned me, asking if I was truly meant to reach that part of the river. I told him that if I got in, there would be no way of controlling the raft, and I had no idea what was beyond the bend. That's when it clicked… I'll say it again: there would be no way of controlling the raft. The Lord stirred my heart, and I understood that was exactly what he wanted. I had to let go of control, forget where I thought I needed to be, and trust that he would guide my boat down the river to where he knew it needed to be.

Who is in control, my friends? We love to hold on to our dreams so tightly, or even say no because they are uncomfortable. We haven't even mentioned the potential of failure yet. Let's talk about that for a minute. I'm certain you've all seen the motivational videos that highlight famous people who failed before making it. Well, I'm going to remind you. Michael Jordan was cut from his high school basketball team. Walt Disney was fired from his job at the newspaper because he lacked ideas. The Beatles were turned down by nearly every record company and were told that boy guitar bands were on their way out. J. K. Rowling was rejected by twelve publishers and was told not to quit her day job.

I've read through countless stories like this, and do you know what stands out? These people didn't let the rejection get to them. They didn't quit; they knew what they had. Do you know what you have? Sometimes these failures shape our visions and dreams into what we really need. Think about how a pearl is formed over time. What starts out as a piece of sand agitating an oyster becomes something beautiful. We must try and fail, then try again. When Thomas Edison was asked about his initial light bulb failures, he responded by saying, "I've tried everything. I have not failed. I have just found ten thousand ways that won't work!"[1]

Can you imagine what our world would look like if dreamers

---

1 | Sarett, L. H. "Research and Invention." *Proceedings of the National Academy of Sciences of the United States of America* 80, no. 14 (1983): 4572–74.

stopped after their first failure? That's a world I wouldn't want to live in. We need more people in our world who continue pursuing their dreams no matter the cost. Great things come from ordinary people. Let's start encouraging people to dream again. To do that, I want to help you move past any obstacles that are keeping you from dreaming, even if the obstacle is yourself. Look inward and begin to search your heart to make sure you aren't holding yourself back or allowing fear to control your creative pursuit.

At the end of each chapter there is an opportunity to reflect, meditate, and pray. Today's prayer will require a little more time and effort. I really don't want you to skip out on it because I think the Lord has something unique he wants to say to you. Early on in this chapter, we talked about our childlike imagination and how there may have been a point at which we stopped dreaming. We all have things that stop us from using our creativity (or at least pursuing it fully). Some have old wounds, some compare themselves to others, and some don't believe in themselves. Regardless of your background, occupation, or skills, you were born to dream and the Lord gave you dreams for a reason.

You were born to dream! As we go into this prayer time, I want you to begin to pray and think through anything that is holding you back. Do you have any memories that pop up? I'll go first. I went to a men's breakfast at our old church shortly after getting married. I hardly knew anyone, as we had just moved to a new town. I struck up a conversation with an older gentleman. He told me about his career then proceeded to ask me what I did. I told him that I was a filmmaker. He smiled and said that was cool, but he wanted to know what I did for a living. I told him again that I worked in the film industry. I guess being from Colorado, it's not something you normally hear. He continued to question me, asking if I was able to actually provide for my wife working in the creative world. I humbly told him that the business had its ups and downs, but yes, I could provide for my wife.

When I think about this memory, it still stings a little and I'm willing to bet that several of you may have experienced something similar. Maybe a comment from a parent, teacher, leader, or friend cut you. I'm not here to tell you that the wounds aren't real. We aren't going to deny their existence. What we are going to do is give them to God. I want you to imagine you're holding an empty box. One by one, I want you to start placing those memories in the box. You can visualize the memories however you want; some people like to imagine them as little stones, some as VHS tapes—you do you. Continue to fill your box up until you've run out of all the memories that have hindered your creative dreams and skills. When you think you've got them all, place them on the steps of the throne of God. You're going to feel the weight lift off your shoulders as you release them. You weren't meant to carry those words. They belong at his feet, fully surrendered.

26

REFLECT AND MEDITATE

I encourage you to get alone and seek the Lord's face. Think about everything you've read in this chapter. What is the Lord speaking to you? I've written some questions below and provided two Bible verses to help guide your quiet reflection with the Lord.

Reflect

What is holding me back from pursuing my creativity?

What areas do I need to experience healing in?

Have I given all this negativity to the Lord?

Is there anything I am doing to sabotage my dreams or skills?

Meditate

Ephesians 2:10: "For we are his workmanship, created in Christ Jesus for good works, which God prepared before that we would walk in them."

1 Peter 5:6-7: "Humble yourselves therefore under the mighty hand of God, that he may exalt you in due time, casting all your worries on him, because he cares for you.

Prayer

Lord, I surrender these things I've been carrying to you. These past wounds aren't bringing life to my skills and talents. I ask that you would heal me from them. I cast these cares and worries on you, Lord. I want to be free from the shame holding me back. I ask forgiveness for holding on to these and wearing them as an identity for too long; they don't belong to me. Thank you for your grace and unending love. I receive a new identity in you. I open myself up to fresh visions and dreams from you, free from the chains that once held me back. I love you, Lord, and I surrender myself to your plans. Amen.

Use this space to write, sketch and respond to the Lord.

3

EXCELLENCE
IN CHRISTIANITY

I'm going to open this chapter with a controversial opinion. I believe we've become complacent with mediocre art in the faith world. Before you write me off completely, I want you to sit with that for a minute. At some point in history, we as Christians started accepting a lower standard for our art, our projects, and our creativity. The phrase "good enough" floats around more often than I care to admit. Don't get me wrong, there are outliers who are setting new trends and making waves, but they will only be a minority unless we do something about it. I believe excellence in creative arts for Christians is imperative.

I know this chapter will rub many folks the wrong way, and I've been praying a lot about this section of the book... Let me make myself perfectly clear: I won't spend time talking about the bad. I will acknowledge that I find myself frustrated with how my fellow Christian artists are settling for substandard art. If you're like me, you may find yourself with that same gut feeling, the one that says, "We can do better." I truly believe that the Lord is going to restore excellent art once again, but that's for the next chapter. Right now, I want to explore the great Christian artists and dreamers throughout history that changed the world with their arts and the standard of excellence they pursued.

For this chapter, I want to take you on a journey through time. Genesis 1:31 says, "God saw everything that he had made, and, behold, it was very good." That second to last word, "very" may also be translated "supremely" or "exceedingly." Creation was more than just good. I can testify to that; our world is amazing and magnificent. There is a YouTube channel called People Are Awesome, where the editing team compiles videos of people accomplishing the impossible. I can't help but watch those videos and think of how much glory that brings to God. He created you and me. And we're not just good, we're very, supremely, exceedingly good. I want you to think about that anytime you feel down or want to give up. The God of the universe created you and said *you are more than good.* Can you imagine if the Lord stopped creating at just good or—even worse—just okay? But the good news is, he didn't. He placed the stars in the sky and the flowers in the field. Nature is beautiful, and he created it all.

Moving forward from Genesis, I want to highlight King David's psalms and music. The lyrics that this man wrote are still changing people's lives today. Think about how often you see a psalm written on a wall, a tattoo, or a bumper sticker. This dude poured his heart and soul into each verse, and it shows. Take a minute to thumb through Psalms at some point today and think about the pure artistry spilling out of that book. David had an amazing anointing; he was a man after God's own heart. In 1 Samuel 16, Saul was troubled with evil spirits, and all it took was David and his harp to free Saul of his spiritual bondage. Think about that for a second. Music brought spiritual freedom. Let me phrase that differently: worship and art were brought into a spiritual battle, and they won. Your art wages war on the enemy; every dream, every vision, scares the darkness and cannot be overcome. Let that encourage you! When you feel discouraged about your gifts, there's a good chance that means that they're working; discouragement and condemnation don't come from our Heavenly Father.

Next in line, we have King Solomon. You may say it was in his genes, but he had a supernatural wisdom beyond comprehension. The Lord offered him any gift he could imagine, and the man chose wisdom because he wanted to make good decisions for his people. How many of us would ask for wisdom when offered riches, fame, and glory? This may seem like a deviation from our creative talk, but I assure you, it's not. Being wise is a gift that should not go unnoticed. We talked about dreamers in the last chapter who were wise—folks like Thomas Edison. God grants wisdom as a gift that can be used to create the unbelievable. Solomon built the temple full of splendor and beauty. If you're not the artsy type and find yourself reading this book, this part is for you. Your mind is a gift that shouldn't go untapped.

Let's jump out of the Bible and move forward to the 1500s. Michelangelo's paintings, sculptures, and art are considered some of the greatest in the world. Hundreds of artists credit him as their source of inspiration and motivation. Did you know that his painting *The Creation of Adam* is one of the most replicated

"WHAT EVER YOU DO
WORK WITH All YOUR
HEART"

COLOSSIANS 3:23

paintings in the world?[2] People look at the Sistine Chapel ceiling and can't help but stand in awe of its greatness. I don't want to bore you with history lessons, but I am trying to make a point; this art was divinely inspired. The stories emanating from his art bring glory to his inspiration, the God of the universe, Creator of heaven and earth.

This inspiration isn't limited to visual art. George Frideric Handel is considered one of the greatest composers of all time. Bach, Beethoven, and even Mozart all admired his talent and spoke highly of him.[3] Nearly three hundred years later, Handel's *Messiah* is still being performed by orchestras globally and can be recognized almost instantly upon its chorus of "Hallelujah." God's fingerprints are all over that song, and people can't help but feel moved as they listen.

Now, I know all these forms of art we just discussed explicitly display Christ, whether as a painted Bible story, a sculpture of a Christian figure, or a song that tells the story of the Messiah. But what about people that took their faith and creativity and made something new and special? Let me tell you about the Inklings. Some of you may know exactly what I'm referring to. Both C. S. Lewis and J. R. R. Tolkien, famed authors, were a part of this legendary writing group at the University of Oxford in the early 1900s. They would get together at the Eagle and Child pub, or "The Bird and Baby" as they called it, to discuss their various fantasy projects. The famous works of fiction penned by these authors include *The Lord of the Rings* and *The Chronicles*

2 | "20 of the World's Most Famous Art Pieces - History Lists," n.d.
3 | Wyn Jones, David "Beethoven's Favourite Composer: George Frideric Handel."

of Narnia. Depending on how you were raised, your family may have had strong feelings for or against these fantasy series, or maybe your family just didn't care. However, when reading these books or watching the film adaptations, Christian allegories and faith elements are undeniable. These two men created entire worlds, languages, and civilizations; they've entertained the masses while introducing Christian themes (some more overt than others).

At some point between the twentieth and twenty-first centuries, some Christian artists began to shift away from publicly displayed Christian themes to allegories. As our world grew darker and continued to reject Christ, faith-based art took a hit. Christian art was beginning to see a decline in consumption. There were phenomenal movies like *Ben-Hur* and *The Ten Commandments*, but after that, something changed. A divide grew in entertainment, where you were no longer simply a musician or a filmmaker. Christians were branded, and their art was branded as well. I'm not saying this is a bad thing, but Christian art was now held to a different standard. Creatives who loved Jesus had their art labeled accordingly. By no means am I saying that Christians should be ashamed of their belief and subsequently their art, but a new genre was created specifically for Christians in all forms of art and media; they were no longer judged by the same criteria as the rest of the arts.

This is the part that can get controversial, so bear with me. We've created a huge divide between Christian and secular entertainment. This divide has pushed both sides away from each other, so much so that neither side wants anything to do with the other. Secular pieces continue to thrive at the box office and on the record charts, while a lot of Christian pieces struggle. Let me clarify, there are phenomenal Christian movies and songs. However, I've personally witnessed a justification taking place. Comments like "It's just a church piece" or "We need to support this because it's Christian" are beginning to sting. I'm really struggling with this, and I'm sure you are too if you're reading this book. Do we have to support certain entertainment just because it's labeled as Christian? Let's look back to guys like the Inklings, who created entire worlds in literature while also challenging each other to do better. While they knew their identity and their faith, they also knew that art at its core is created to entertain and inspire.

We've got a "message versus story" problem in the faith-based entertainment world. Here's the hang-up I'm seeing: most Christian projects are built around a particular message that they are trying to convey, then they figure out how to fit it into a story. Any audience can see right through that. We need to be okay telling stories first and allowing the message to come second. Disclaimer: Hollywood definitely has messages and agendas in their media, but generally the story is what determines whether it gets made. Secular entertainers are writing films and letting their morals dictate their boundaries, goals, and mission behind it. Hollywood sees the value and return when they make movies that reflect reality rather than push an agenda. What if we started telling amazing stories that are shaped by our morals instead of shoehorning a story into a message?

There is a general fear that if Christian content has anything controversial, it will be boycotted or canceled. I've sat in meetings where producers ask the directors to remove any references to alcohol, drugs, or sex because it's not appropriate. Don't get me wrong, I don't think any of those things should be glorified in a film, and some people can get caught up in adding gratuitous scenes just for the sake of being dangerous and edgy. However, if your character is a prodigal, why avoid an alcohol reference if it serves the story? Sometimes Christian entertainment is so concerned with making material more palatable for their audience that they water it down until there's no truth left to tell.

Have you ever taken a moment to think about the parables in the Bible? The parable of the good Samaritan tells the story of a man who is beaten and bloodied. Both a priest and Levite leave him for dead, but he is helped by a man who, in any other circumstance, would have been expected to kill him. The parable of the prodigal son is about a son who takes half of his father's belongings and dives headlong into greed, gambling, and debauchery.

As Christians, we need to be okay with being honest and telling stories that are real. We can't make shallow art. It's time for a new level of excellence. Times are changing and so are we. There is a glimmer of light on the horizon. The Lord is raising up new creatives that are challenging the system and shaking things up.

But more on that in the next chapter. For now, I want to wrap this up; I don't want you to feel disheartened by any of this. If anything, I want you to feel encouraged and inspired. Some of the artists that may have come to your mind while reading this aren't doing anything wrong. They are making movies for specific audiences and succeeding. They are called to make Christian movies and they are getting better. My question to you is this: Who is the audience that the Lord has called you to? We are going to touch more on that later, but start mulling it over. For now, I've left you some prayer points to think about, and I will see you in the next chapter.

REFLECT AND MEDITATE

I encourage you to get alone and seek the Lord's face. Think about everything you've read in this chapter. What is the Lord speaking to you? I've written some questions below and provided two Bible verses to help guide your quiet reflection with the Lord.

Reflect

How is my creativity supposed to look different?

How can I pursue creative excellence?

What skills do I need to grow in to be the best at my craft?

Are my dreams limited by my skill sets?

Meditate

Colossians 3:23: "And whatever you do, work heartily, as for the Lord, and not for men."

Philippians 4:8: "Finally, brothers, whatever things are true, whatever things are honorable, whatever things are just, whatever things are pure, whatever things are lovely, whatever things are of good report: if there is any virtue and if there is any praise, think about these things."

Prayer

Lord, you've created me to pursue excellence. Help me to grow and learn. I ask for new opportunities to increase my skill sets. I want to bring glory to you in everything I do. I ask that you would allow me to honor and respect the dreamers that have gone before me. I apologize for any negativity I may have toward the current state of creativity in the faith world. You are the Creator of creativity and I'm blessed to be a part of it. I love you, Lord; thank you for all you are doing! Amen.

Use this space to write, sketch and respond to the Lord.

4

A Fresh Creative Awakening

Well, I'm glad you came back! Sometimes when I talk about the current state of Christian entertainment, it gets a little controversial. In no way do I ever want to speak poorly of anyone's art or talents. As Christians, we are called to come alongside one another to encourage, not criticize, and to challenge, not condemn. I think we've been seeing a lack of both—or at least disunity.

Last chapter, we looked at pieces in history that exemplified excellence. So where do we go from here? It's a great question, and I'm glad you asked. I think before we run ahead and look to the future, we need to honor the present-day Christians that are giving secular artists a run for their money. Movies like *Jesus Revolution* and television shows like *The Chosen* are great examples of filmmakers that know their stuff. Both production companies tell amazing stories and execute high-value productions. This isn't something Christian audiences have seen much of in the past, but this is exactly what we need. They are setting new trends in Hollywood, and let me tell you, even non-Christian crew members are starting to take notice. I have several friends who worked for the producers above, and they are actively choosing to work on these projects for several reasons. Let's dive into what they are doing right.

First off, both production companies have chosen to focus on good storytelling. They figured out what stories needed to be told and how to best tell them. I can guarantee that every single project these guys are working on starts with a logline—a one-to-two-sentence story summary—which is then built into a script that follows the classic three-act structure of every good story. A character goes through some kind of experience that results in them being changed in some kind of way. The difference between these stories and others that are hard to watch is that they aren't letting the moral they'd like to teach or the message they'd like to preach take center stage. Instead, they do everything they can to simply tell a good story well, and their message and morals are a part of how they achieve that.

This leads me to the next success point: morals. These production teams have standards on their sets and throughout their projects that are different from those of Hollywood. I've heard from plenty of crew that have worked with the various faith-based directors and producers above; they are being Christ on set. They are known for their love, and treating their crews better than a standard Hollywood production. Hopefully it encourages you to hear that. As a producer, that is something I've tried to be so intentional about.

I produced a project years ago on the West Coast, and we had an actress that was part of the LGBTQ+ community. At the beginning she was a little apprehensive about coming onto a Christian set. She was uncertain about how she would be treated. Her acting skills were off the charts. We had hired her for a specific character, and she nailed it. When we wrapped the project, she noted how well she had been treated, even better than on secular sets. Those types of moments continue to reaffirm for me the good we are bringing to the film community. Oftentimes, Christians in film think that they are representing Christ through the screen, but that's not always the case. Sometimes we're called to make a movie for a secular audience and allow the *crew* to experience God *behind* the camera. Remember that when you think about the industry: some Christian filmmakers are called to impact the audience, but you can make a much more personal impact on those you work with behind the scenes.

Finally, the last film point I want to discuss is production value. Bad quality is found everywhere—in both Christian *and* secular art—but what separates the good from the bad in terms of excellence? The producers highlighted above all know and understand the need for good lighting, cinematography, acting, set design, music, and more. If even one of those things is skipped, it's immediately noticeable and lessens the experience and impact of the end product. As we mentioned before, hold your craft to a high standard. Pursue quality and don't cut corners.

Obviously, I love to talk about films. It's my wheelhouse. But let's jump out of the film world and apply this to the music industry. There are amazing musicians and artists who love

Jesus, and their content shows it. The rap community is thriving under Lecrae's Reach Records team, and guys like NF are beyond skilled at adding music to that genre that brings meaning and lacks profanity. Both of these rap groups aren't always preaching: sometimes they are telling a story, sometimes they are sharing their struggles in life… They are being authentic, and their audience responds to it.

What about bands like Switchfoot? They are a phenomenal rock band that has mastered their lyrics and music. They regularly play sold-out shows in huge venues all around the world. Their music attracts audiences from all backgrounds, yet they never settle for anything less than their best. While they aren't shy about their belief in God, they stick to their morals and make amazing music.

So what am I getting at here? Well, I've hopefully started painting a picture for you of the modern-day artists that are thriving and succeeding. As we've gone through their works, we can learn from their talents and apply them to our own. If you walk away from this chapter with anything, I hope it is this: we are called to be excellent artists that tell good stories, add production value, and treat people differently. This book is preparing you for something bigger, friend. I've said it before, your dreams are important and have value. Each chapter will continue to add tools, wisdom, and skills to your belt.

Looking forward, we see there is a new wave of creativity falling on the church. This is why this next season is pivotal. New creatives have been anointed and called to challenge the Christian media system and make excellent art. Colossians 3:23 says, "And whatever you do, work heartily, as for the Lord, and not

I WILL POUR MY SPIRIT
OUT ON ALL FLESH
ACTS 2:17

for men." That, my friends, is what's happening. Creatives are putting their whole hearts forward for the Lord and not trying to please men (their audience). When we do that, something changes and our art takes on a whole new level of skill.

Clearly this is something I'm passionate about. We founded Parable International with one main vision: train the body of Christ to pursue excellence in creativity and the arts. We sold our house and gave up a comfortable lifestyle for something bigger than ourselves. I'm not saying this to toot my own horn, but because I want you to understand that this is something my family is actively working on, every day and everywhere. For the last two years, we've traveled from city to city to come alongside countless ministries, help them assess their current creative vision, then equip them to grow in their skills and talents. The workers are there, and you're one of them… They aren't lacking people; they are lacking the skill sets or even just the time to reach their vision. If that's you, I want to encourage you to put in your ten thousand hours, hone your craft, and seek greatness and quality.

Our goal with Parable is to train and launch the best creatives this world has even seen. This is an audacious goal no doubt, but set your sights high and aim for the stars, my friend. I've got to practice what I preach. We started on the road because we heard the Lord clearly ask us to go out on mission, find the ministries that want training, and help bring fresh creative vision. And the resulting season has been so sweet. Difficult, for sure, but beautiful. My wife, kids, and I have traveled the world, learned phrases in different languages to get by in other countries, and made friends in so many different cities. We've chosen to get uncomfortable because this is a vision I believe in with every ounce of my being. The coolest part is that we are beginning to see fruits of the seeds we started planting several years ago. Ministries are thriving in their creativity, resulting in a larger reach for their mission.

We know this season of full-time travel is just that, a season. At some point, we will come off the road, and begin sowing into a community and cultivating artists that produce excellence. We want to see new creatives operating in the entertainment industry (both secular and Christian), the ministry world, and the mission field. Our prayer is that we can train people to exemplify good moral character and fine-tune their craft.

We have huge dreams and aspirations. I want to flood the industry with excellent filmmakers that won't stop at just creating good art. For all you non-film people, I hope that this chapter didn't bore you. I do hope that you can take what you're reading here and apply it to your own career. At the end of the day, all our work fields could use fresh vision, fresh wind, and inspiration. Take this newfound pursuit of excellence and apply it to your hobbies or in your office. Don't just stop when you think the task is sufficiently done, take the extra step and complete it in excellence.

As I'm writing this, I realize I keep using the word *excellence*. But let me assure you, I don't use it lightly. I've spent time poring over synonyms, but I can't even find one suitable alternative. The word *perfection* has come up a few times as a substitute, but it feels weird to tell someone to pursue perfection because there was only one man to walk the earth who was perfect. We can pursue it, but perfection cannot be achieved in the way excellence can.

In my household, we grew up with a phrase that usually puzzled people. When tasked with something, my parents would often ask my brother and I if we "got the message to Garcia." Some of you may have heard about this piece written by Elbert Hubbard in 1899. "A Message to Garcia" is a short essay about President McKinley commissioning a man named Lieutenant Rowan to find General Garcia, who happened to be hiding out somewhere in the jungles of Cuba. The story describes how Rowan took the letter, no questions asked, trudged the jungles of Cuba, and emerged three weeks later having delivered this urgent message. Hubbard talks about the rarity of this kind of character. A man was given a task with only one instruction—get the message to Garcia—and then followed through to completion without any further inquiries or even details. If you ever get a chance, take a minute to read the short essay; it can be found online with a quick search.

I bring this up because this is the type of character that the Lord is looking for. People who will hear his voice and simply say yes, no questions asked. People are quick to ask: Why? How? Can it wait? Where should I go? Is it worth it? Sure, sometimes questions are needed from a vague boss, but are we going the extra mile to accomplish the task in front of us? Chick-fil-A encourages their employees to provide "second mile service." The first mile is expected, but are you going to go above and beyond to deliver more than enough? As we discussed in chapter 3, when

God created us, he said we were very good, more than enough. Are we going to give God more than enough?

I'll leave you with this. You are called and set apart. The Lord has given you dreams and visions for a reason; nothing goes wasted. Some of your gifts and talents may not make sense right now, but I promise they belong. He is preparing you for a new season, one where you are going to experience new fruit and fresh wind. I pray that as you read this, something in your spirit is leaping. If you've got a burning desire to change the world, know that it starts with your current environment. Sow into the season and atmosphere you're in; it may change over time, but just be present. The Lord sees you and has his hand over your life. Things may not always go as planned, but look for him in those situations. He never left your side. Life is difficult, friends; we live in a fallen world. But as long as we keep our focus on the Lord, he *will* make our paths straight. Keep fighting the good fight.

REFLECT AND MEDITATE

I encourage you to get alone and seek the Lord's face. Think about everything you've read in this chapter. What is the Lord speaking to you? I've written some questions below and provided two Bible verses to help guide your quiet reflection with the Lord.

Reflect

How can I add value to my creativity?

Are there stories I need to tell?

As an artist, am I representing Christ to those around me?

Am I "getting the message to Garcia"?

Meditate

Acts 2:17: "It will be in the last days, says God, that I will pour out my Spirit on all flesh. Your sons and your daughters will prophesy. Your young men will see visions. Your old men will dream dreams."

Matthew 6:10: "Let your Kingdom come. Let your will be done on earth as it is in heaven."

Prayer

Father, I come to you right now and ask for fresh vision. You're waking up new dreamers, and I know that I'm a part of that movement. Here I am, Lord, send me. I ask that you would use my hands to bring glory to you both in my art and in my character. I am humbled to be chosen by you and thankful for you in my life. Thank you, Lord, for your daily grace and wisdom. I surrender my own thoughts and ideas to you. You are so good, Father. Amen.

Use this space to write, sketch and respond to the Lord.

5

WHERE DO I FIT IN?

We live in a world in an identity crisis. Our young ones are inundated with talk of who they should and shouldn't be when they grow up. My hope is that in this chapter, we can talk about our identities and how we can align them with the Lord by releasing our rights and submitting our plans to Him. In the past few chapters, I've provided some tools to help you become the best version of yourself. I've talked about hearing the Lord's voice, encouraged you to dream again, and discussed excellence in past, present, and future entertainment. So where do you fit in?

To figure that out, let's dig deep and go through an exercise that might help. Imagine you're sitting in a living room full of decorations and furniture. Each piece in the room represents part of your identity. The pictures on the walls display various talents, and the furniture is crafted by memories that make up who you are today. One by one, we are going to strip them away.

I want to get to your core. If we take away all these physical things that represent your personality and your story, where do we land? Slowly each item in the room begins to fade until you're left standing in an empty room. It's just you now, before your gifts, dreams, and talents. Who are you in that moment?

Jeremiah 1:5 says, "Before I formed you in the womb, I knew you. Before you were born, I sanctified you." Think about this for a second: the Creator of the universe knew you before you were even formed. Before you became you, he knew where you were going and what you were destined for. Way back before that living room was furnished, he called you his. The word *knew* derives from the Hebrew word *yâda* (יָדַע), which literally means to know on a level of intimate depth.

Psalm 139:13-14 says, "For you formed my inmost being. You knit me together in my mother's womb. I will give thanks to you, for I am fearfully and wonderfully made." Hopefully both of these verses paint a new picture for you: you are God's. He created you, and he placed a purpose on your life. If we peel back the layers of your history and experience, your identity first lies in Christ. Don't ever forget that. Make sure you lean into that in times of uncertainty. We look at our dreams and sometimes question if we have what it takes. The truth is our flesh doesn't. We will fail over and over again if we rely on our own strength because we were never made to do it alone. We were with him in the beginning, but at some point we thought we could do it without him. News flash: We can try, but the results are going to be disappointing.

Over the years, as we began to learn new talents or discover our gifts, some of us forgot where they came from. The good news is that the Bible tells us exactly where they come from. James 1:17 says, "Every good gift and every perfect gift is from above, coming down from the Father of lights." Well, that was easy. The verse leaves little to decipher. Unfortunately, we live in a world that tries to distort that belief and convince you that you need to do more and work harder to achieve success. Society tries to define our value and self-worth by what we can provide. Our gifts can get belittled or—even worse—elevated and idolized. People with notable talent are worshiped on screen and stage. We're told they are the models of success. This is false on so many levels. We need to reject this lie; our value is not determined by any amount of success. Anytime you begin to feel down about your dreams or accomplishments, repeat that well-known worship lyric: "I am who he says I am."

Now that we've established who you are in Christ, let's take a look in your toolbox. What are the gifts, talents, dreams, and visions God has given you? Some of you may see all sorts of artsy stuff, others may see more technical or intellectual stuff. Regardless of what tools you see in there, they are all there for a reason. The Lord lets nothing go to waste. Let me give you an example.

When I was in high school, my dad made me take a graphic design class. I was frustrated because I thought it was pointless. I told him that it wouldn't help me with my theater career... Yes, I thought I was going to go into musical theater. This was before I heard the Lord tell me to get behind the camera, and I am so grateful I listened. Anyway, my dad had me take the elective because he knew I could be good at it and it would also give us opportunities to work together in his printing business. As years went by and I pursued my film career, I started to use

① IN All YOUR WAYS ACKNOWLEDGE →HIM←

② AND HE will MAKE YOUR PATH STRAIGHT

→PROVERBS← 3:6

graphic design to market my films, but I never thought much of it. I never considered myself to be a designer. Fast-forward to the launch of our ministry; a missions organization asked if we could also host a few graphics classes in addition to our film training. That's when it hit me: I had spent years developing these various skills, all of which seemed to be completely unrelated until I began to put together curriculum for our training programs and workshops. By no means am I an expert in graphic design, but I had the tools necessary to teach photo editing, logo design, and the basics. I look back on my jobs in print shops, photography gigs, journalism internships, and I see that the Lord was preparing me for this.

So what is he preparing you for? I mentioned early on that my hope is that by the time you set this book down, you have a dream that is burning in your heart, one that can't be ignored. He's given you everything you need, and maybe he's highlighting some new skill sets as well. As you're thinking about this from (hopefully) a fresh perspective, we need to set some ground rules that should result in success.

Have you ever heard of the concept of releasing your rights? You may have heard it in a legal setting or maybe at youth camp years ago. I remember so vividly the first time I heard a message about relinquishing our rights to the Lord. At first, it didn't make sense, but as I let it sit, it began to sting, but I got it. This concept is very countercultural. The world tells us that we deserve things simply because we are living. I'm not talking about basic human rights; those are great and make total sense, but they don't belong in this context. Oftentimes, we look at our giftings and callings as rights. While we may not ever verbalize this, we feel that we are entitled to them, that we somehow earned them or own them.

Obviously, I am making a blanket statement and not all of you fall into this category. Regardless, if that's you or not, I want you to pick out just one skill you have, think about it, and now imagine what it would feel like if it was taken from you in an instant. Who would you be without it? How would you feel? For some folks, this has actually happened due to an accident or loss. People can be thrust into deep depression because of this very situation. This happens when we place all our hope and trust in something that is temporary. I'd like to challenge you to begin thinking about your abilities differently. Our talents, dreams, and visions are gifts, just as it says in James 1:17, which I referenced earlier. Gifts are something we don't deserve or earn, yet they are given to us by our Creator. Start to look at them as gifts to be stewarded rather than things you deserve. You've been entrusted with something precious from the Lord, but have you trusted him with it in return?

I want you to imagine that you are holding a piece of cookie dough. Now, for this illustration, we have to pretend that most of us don't eat raw cookie dough, even though it's delicious. This cookie dough is different though, it's your calling, made up of gifts and talents given to you by the Lord. He's given you all the right ingredients and asked you to steward it well. Now, this piece of cookie dough is still raw; for it to reach its fullness, you've got to put it in the oven. So you open the oven and stick your hand in, right? No! You place it on a baking sheet and put it in the preheated oven. If you're not willing to release the dough and trust the oven to do its job, you're going to run into a few issues. First off, you're going to burn your hand, and it's not going to feel great. Second, by holding on to that dough, you are hindering the process—your flesh is getting in the way and that dough will never reach its full potential as a cooked dessert.

If you're not picking up what I'm laying down, let me explain it another way. The Lord has given you a calling, a dream, a vision… All are gifts from him, but you've got to reciprocate that trust. He gives us these things, and we love to hold on so tightly to them. Don't get me wrong, they have value and because of that, we need to trust the Lord in return with them.

Proverbs 3:5-6 says, "Trust in Yahweh with all your heart, and don't lean on your own understanding. In all your ways acknowledge him, and he will make your paths straight." This verse says to trust the Lord with just some of your heart, right? No… He says trust him with *all* your heart. Don't try to do it yourself. Seek him in *all* things, and he *will* make your paths straight. Okay, Tyler, you've made your point, trust is important, but what does that truly look like?

The word you are looking for is *surrender*. When I hear this word, I always think back to a message I heard in my early teen years. Our pastor was talking about why we raise our hands in worship. He said that when we raise our hands, we are making ourselves vulnerable and open; we've got nothing to hide. He compared it to when a child lifts their arms to their parents; they want to be held, so they are surrendering themselves to be carried in the arms of their loved one. Are we able to position our hearts to be completely at the mercy of our Heavenly Father?

When we submit our lives, our desires, and every aspect of our being to the Lord, something is bound to happen. I remember as a teen, sitting in a discipleship class and hearing our leader talk about how important it is to submit all things to the Lord.

We were asked to open our journals and make a list of everything we thought we needed in our lives: skills, careers, relationships, success, and anything else. He challenged us to take the list seriously, pray over it, and give it all to God. Not just by our words but by lifestyle. I so clearly remember him telling us not to take this lightly; we needed to be so content with giving each item to the Lord that if any one of those things on the list was taken, we would still be at peace. You might say that's impossible, and it is very difficult, but it can be done. So we wrote our lists and started offering these desires to God. We worked toward being so content in our relationship with him that nothing else could even come close. Pursue the cross and the things of this world will surely fade away.

So after the discipleship program, I continued this journey of surrender and submission to the Lord. At the top of my list, I had three items: buy a car, graduate college debt-free, and meet the woman of my dreams. I would pray every day and say, "Lord, I give you my desires. I give you the right to own a car, I give you the right to graduate from college debt-free, and I give you the right to be in a relationship with the woman of my dreams." You see, when I started this prayer journey, these desires weren't yet fulfilled, but they were the deepest wants in my life at the time. Slowly but surely, when I had finally reached the point where I was content with or without each of those things, the Lord deemed me ready. This wasn't an overnight process; this took years and a lot of effort to release my rights to him. I still remember each moment I was gifted with the fulfillment of those desires.

The car came first. I was working in youth ministry and had finally accepted the fact that I may have to drive my mother's red minivan every day. I stopped looking for a car and told the Lord that the search was in his hands, not mine. I couldn't afford anything more than $600, which even fifteen years ago wouldn't buy you anything. One day, I got a call from my grandfather who ran a mechanic shop. He told me he had an old car that someone was willing to part with for $600 if I was interested. And just like that, I purchased my 1991 Subaru Legacy. She wasn't perfect, but she was mine!

My university was next on the list. I got accepted into a school that I couldn't afford. I applied to every scholarship and even got quite a few, but I still came up short for my housing finances. I remember sitting down and saying, "Lord, I can't afford this school, and I know this is small, but I surrender the right to go to this college." As the summer came to an end, I had explored every option to obtain additional finances for school and had resolved that I most likely would be unable to attend. I had reached a contentment that maybe it wasn't something the Lord wanted for me, and then I got a call about an RA job at the school that had just opened up. I was told that normally they wouldn't offer the position to a transfer student, but with my experience working with graduate students in a past job, they wanted to know if I would consider working for the graduate housing community while attending undergraduate school; in exchange, I would receive an apartment for my time! I spent the remainder of my time in school doing that job and graduated debt-free a few years later.

Finally, the last and most important thing—or person—on this list. I so deeply wanted to find a wife and get married to someone who knew the Lord and could love me well. I spent several years praying over this and tried to figure out how to give up pursuing a relationship with someone I had never met yet. The Lord continued to have me focus my eyes on him. The college years can make a dude go crazy when he is avoiding the dating scene until the Lord tells him otherwise. The more time I spent with the Lord, the less I looked for Mrs. Right. Then one day, my dad told me about his friend's daughter. He told me she loved Jesus and loved missions, and he thought I would find her attractive. In all seriousness, I laughed it off and told him I wasn't looking to be in a relationship. I said that I was excited about everything the Lord was doing in my life and didn't need any distractions. Well, I definitely put my foot in my mouth… When I saw her picture, I knew there was something different about her. This woman was radiant and beautiful, and she literally checked everything off my wants and needs list (remember that from youth group?). It took some time, but when we finally met, I heard this whisper, "This is who you've been waiting for." Whew, I get emotional just thinking about the moment I first saw her. Something in my heart leapt, and I knew that I knew she was the one.

I share this to hopefully illustrate that when you fully submit your plans to the Lord, he delivers. Now, these are only three on a list of quite a few things. There were definitely desires on my list that God never fulfilled, but I'm okay with that. I learned to focus on the right things. Sometimes we have seasons where we are headed in one direction, and in the next season the Lord changes the wind. That is okay, and we need to take it as it comes. Trust the Lord's process; it is so much better than anything we could ever ask for. I'll leave you with this. I am so glad my visions are not my own and this ministry isn't mine. These skills are a blessing, but I'm just a vessel. If I ever tried to do this on my own, I'd fail time and time again. I'm grateful for God's grace and for the opportunity to steward these dreams each day he returns them to me.

REFLECT AND MEDITATE

I encourage you to get alone and seek the Lord's face. Think about everything you've read in this chapter. What is the Lord speaking to you? I've written some questions below and provided three Bible verses to help guide your quiet reflection with the Lord.

Reflect

Who does the Lord say I am?

How does my flesh get in the way?

What does daily submission look like?

Am I willing to release my rights?

Meditate

Jeremiah 1:5: "Before I formed you in the womb, I knew you. Before you were born, I sanctified you."

James 1:17: "Every good gift and every perfect gift is from above, coming down from the Father of lights."

Proverbs 3:5-6: "Trust in Yahweh with all your heart, and don't lean on your own understanding. In all your ways acknowledge him, and he will make your paths straight."

Prayer

Lord, I come to you and ask you to empty me. I choose you and your plans for my life. Help me learn to submit all of my ways to you. You've given me purpose and called me your own. Help me seek you and deny my flesh. I love you, Lord. Thank you for your goodness in my life. Amen.

Side note: If you just finished this chapter, there is an exercise on the next page. I recommend doing this while the chapter is fresh.

Your Submission List

Congratulations! You made it halfway through the book. If you just finished the last chapter, there's no better time to put submission into practice. Put on some worship music, grab something to write with, and begin to scribble down your list. Ask the Lord what you need to surrender. What skills, talents, dreams, and visions do you need to lay down? I encourage you to write them all out; leave no rock unturned. My list had my spouse all the way down to my clothing choices. Take this seriously. And save the list! Take a picture of it and hold on to it. Proceed to pray over each item and present it to the Lord. Place them all at his feet and pursue the cross.

Use this space to write, sketch and respond to the Lord.

6

CREATE FOR HIS GLORY

This chapter, in all honesty, was probably the hardest to write. I've started to write this opening paragraph over and over again, more times than I care to admit. I sense that the Lord has a lot for you here; take your time and open your heart to what he wants to speak over you and your art.

We, as Christians, struggle with an internal conflict. I've seen it divide production companies and churches alike. While we identify ourselves in Christ, we wrestle with balancing our beliefs and our creativity in our work. Sometimes, we struggle with labeling our art as Christian or not and even feel pressure to conform to a certain message. I want to address these things and explore fresh ways to look at them with the Lord.

I want to start off by saying that it is important to remember that our identity is found in Christ, not in our art. We talked a lot about identity in the last chapter. With that being said, the Lord is undeniably in our lives. He lives in us, inspires us, and is in everything we do. While our identity in the Lord isn't something that always affects our outward appearance, it's always there. Let's take this concept and apply it to our creativity. Sometimes our art outwardly displays a Christian message and sometimes it doesn't, that doesn't change our identity in the Father. Let me tell you a story.

There once was a carpenter who created a beautiful bench. Every part of this piece was a work of art. People would pass by and often comment on its rare beauty. One day, an interested buyer inquired about the woodwork. He asked the carpenter about the process, the type of wood, and the stain. Near the end of the conversation, the man asked one final question that caught the woodworker off guard: "Where's Jesus in this bench?" The carpenter stood in silence for a minute and replied, "He's in me, isn't that good enough?" Quickly the interested buyer fired back, "You are a Christian, correct? Shouldn't there be a verse or cross engraved somewhere in the wood? Your art is either Christian or not."

You see, this story sounds silly and extremely overdramatic... That's the point. I am using this tale to illustrate something that we need to talk about. This is happening on a different type of scale with Christians in entertainment and the arts. Maybe you've experienced this as well. I've had plenty of folks assume that every film I make is Christian because I am. Unfortunately, this is a misconception that we deal with on a regular basis. Our art is forced to choose an identity when it may not have one. Don't get me wrong, there are paintings, songs, and even movies that are clearly created to share the gospel, but it doesn't mean that they glorify God any more or less than wildlife photography or fiction literature. I believe that simply using the gifts he gave us brings him glory. Our gifts and creativity are given to us by God to glorify him, they may not fit into a specific box, and that's okay.

As you begin to reevaluate your art, throw off the boundaries that try and limit it. Freely run toward art and creativity. I think about my daughter and her many drawings that cover our walls and refrigerator. She often hands me a piece of paper with a mermaid or a princess full of colors. As her dad, I love seeing her use her creativity and artistry to make beautiful things. She isn't restricted to a genre or confined to a message she must convey, she simply creates because she can. Is that something we are thinking about when we sit down to create? Step one in this process is to create because you can!

Calling is something we hear tossed around a lot in Christian circles. If you are reading this book, I'm sure creativity plays a large part in your calling. Some of us are called to share the gospel as an outward expression of our art, and others are called to bring the Lord glory in different ways. I get asked a lot by folks about the types of movies and TV shows I work on. People want to know why I pick certain projects and turn others down. Well, let me speak for myself and I will let you decide where you land.

I am called to be a filmmaker who pursues excellence and glorifies God both on-screen and behind the camera. What does that mean? Well, first off, I let my morals dictate the projects I say yes and no to. I have drawn a hard line in the sand, and I avoid certain types of content. I work on movies that may not be Christian, and there may even be content that will challenge viewers, but I'm not saying this to glorify it. I absolutely can't stand gratuitous language or obscene content, nor will I take part in it. But on the flip side, I value truth over palatability and don't ever want to justify watered-down content.

Let me tell you a story that I heard years ago. I can't verify its authenticity but have no doubts that something along these lines happened. Filmmakers were finishing a faith-based film about an individual and their salvation journey. When the first cut of the movie was presented to the executives, they came back and asked the filmmakers to remove the mild drug references because they may be too jarring for the audience. Confused, the director and his editing team obliged and resubmitted the film. Again, the executives came back and asked them to remove the red plastic cups from the party scene because they could possibly have a negative impact on the younger viewers. Frustrated at constant nitpicking and micromanagement, the production team fulfilled the request and presented it a final time. This time the executives assured them they were almost there, but there was a scene where a girl takes the guy by the hand, leads him to a bedroom, and shuts the door; they knew what this was implying and didn't think the audience could handle it. Finally, the director and his team responded rather harshly. He pointed out that the executives were forcing him to water down the content. The executives believed that a Christian audience couldn't handle an authentic story about someone who struggled with substances and relationships. The director called them out and told them that they were doing the film a disservice by pandering to an audience that deserved the truth. This project in no way glorified sin; in fact, it was all about the redemption that this character found when he realized the things of this earth lacked meaning.

WHAT EVER YOU DO — Do All To The Glory Of GOD

I CORINTHIANS 10:31

Every time I think of that story, I get fired up because those conversations happen on a regular basis in Christian production offices around the world. I remember working on a secular project with some amazing people. I read through the script and while there were some cool themes that could be interpreted as Christian, it was a pretty straightforward good-guy-versus-the-villain movie. I had a family member ask me if there was profanity in the project, and I told them there were a few mild curse words. My family member asked me why I was justifying it. I laugh a little when I think about my response. I told them that the swearing came from the bad guy after he got shot. I mean, what would you say? "Gosh darn it, I've been hit." No, I'm sure you would say some colorful words if you were a villain who had finally been caught. All that to say, no one can tell you what you can and can't be a part of. That is between you and Jesus. Don't ever use comparison to justify a project.

So we've talked about the outward expression of our art that can either be Christian or not, but what about behind the art? Let's switch our view from the art to the artist. How do we bring glory to the Lord in the process of making a project? Well, it starts by modeling Christ as an artist. Regardless of your creative medium, you can reflect Christ in any environment. The entertainment world can be dark, and sometimes people don't treat each other well. I want to encourage you to stand out and invite the Lord into those projects. You may be the only person who is carrying the Holy Spirit into those atmospheres. Don't stoop down to levels below you. In the film world there is a lot of negativity and gossip, but don't get caught up in that; instead, speak life over people. I'm not saying you have to evangelize while you are creating your art (though maybe you do), but just be the person you were created to be without compromise.

As we look inwardly at our hearts, we need to ask the question: Who are we creating for? I once had a Christian filmmaker tell me that we need to check our egos at the door. This is something that will set you apart from secular entertainers. Are we creating for God's glory or ours? I'm reminded of John 1:8, "He was not the light, but was sent that he might testify about the light." The Lord highlighted this verse to me as an artist so long ago. To this day, I am constantly reminded of it. We were created not to be the light, but to reflect it, bear witness to it, and testify of it. Jesus is the light, and we are merely here to be vessels. As we talked in the last chapter, we need to submit ourselves to him and allow him to fill us.

So how can we share this light with others through our creativity? Sometimes it is reflected in our art, and sometimes it's reflected in how we create our art. You need to seek the Lord specifically about your calling in partnership with your creativity. We need to learn to create for an audience of One. Humility is a huge trait that is needed in the creative world. It's so easy to stand on a stage or present a piece of art and receive the glory ourselves. But this will only harm us and hold us back from growing.

Philippians 2:3 says, "Doing nothing through rivalry or through conceit, but in humility, each counting others better than himself." Our pride doesn't belong in our art; this is why submission is key. The more we can release to the Lord, the easier it gets to deflect and reflect. That was a phrase my Bible teacher used to use with us in high school. He would pour into various star athletes and encourage them to deflect the glory and reflect

God's glory. Around that same time in high school, I saw a vision of a mirror on stage. I was struggling with pride a lot in that season, and the Lord was teaching me how to step to the side. The mirror stood on stage and was placed in front of me. The light would come down from the heavens, hit the mirror, and reflect to the audience. I was just there to hold it in place. Are we able to get ourselves to that point in our art?

No one is perfect, my friends. We all look at our art and wonder where it belongs and even where we belong as artists. What circles are we called to impact? We've talked about impacting both our audience and fellow artists around us, but at the end of the day, we are called to create for his glory. With that in mind, I want to challenge you to begin this race with a new outlook about who you are serving with your art. Go forward with this mindset and create, just as the Father intended.

REFLECT AND MEDITATE

I encourage you to get alone and seek the Lord's face. Think about everything you've read in this chapter. What is the Lord speaking to you? I've written some questions below and provided two Bible verses to help guide your quiet reflection with the Lord.

Reflect

Who am I called to be as an artist?

What does it look like to create for the Lord's glory?

Have I found my identity in the Lord or in my art?

Where is the line in the sand that the Lord
is asking me to stand on?

Meditate

1 Corinthians 10:31: "Whether therefore you eat, or drink, or whatever you do, do all to the glory of God."

Matthew 5:14-16: "You are the light of the world. A city located on a hill can't be hidden. Neither do you light a lamp and put it under a measuring basket, but on a stand; and it shines to all who are in the house.

Even so, let your light shine before men, that they may see your good works and glorify your Father who is in heaven."

Prayer

Lord, thank you for calling us to create for your glory. Help me to step to the side and learn to be a vessel for you. I ask that you would speak to me about my art and where it belongs. Thank you for the gifts you've given me and the areas in which I get to serve with them. You are such a good Father. Thank you for the gift of creativity. Help me continue to create, and I ask that you would continue to inspire me. I love you, Jesus. Amen.

Use this space to write, sketch and respond to the Lord.

7

CREATE SPACE
FOR HIM

Dreamer, I'm grinning ear to ear right now. This chapter is the culmination of everything this book stands for, and I can't wait to dive into this content with you. These concepts may not be revolutionary for you, but they were life changing for me, and they dictate every aspect of my own personal creativity.

We're going to start off with a question: Why are we comfortable inviting the Holy Spirit into our churches, finances, ministries, and sports, but we struggle with the idea that he has an interest in the arts or wants to be involved in our creativity? Hopefully, as we have been going through this book, this idea has been already brewing, but now it's undeniable. We ask the Lord to guide us in all aspects of life but often forget to invite him into our creativity and dreams. I'm not just talking about our grand ideas, I'm also talking about your hobbies and skills:

photography, graphic design, writing, painting, sculpting, film-making, music, and all other forms of creating. This also applies to those who are created more technical in nature: programmers, engineers, doctors, scientists, carpenters, accountants, and others. The Lord wants to be involved in everything we do.

Revelation 3:20 says, "Behold, I stand at the door and knock. If anyone hears my voice and opens the door, then I will come in to him, and will dine with him, and he with me." Our Heavenly Father is standing by just waiting to jump at the opportunity to be invited into our creative space. He never forces his way into our projects. He has given us free will, and it's up to us to ask the questions he's eagerly waiting to answer. As a father myself, I know the overwhelming honor and joy I feel when my children ask me to come play with them. Playing with Legos or coloring becomes a highlight of my day, all because my kids care enough to ask their daddy to participate in their creativity. The truth is, if I feel so incredibly full in that moment, how much more is our Heavenly Father eager to join us?

Now, before we dive into the process of inviting the Lord into our creativity, I want to address one more misnomer. The Lord wants to be involved, regardless of the form of art or its genre. Again, our identity is in him, and we allow our identity to shape our morals, but he cares about our art—with or without a message attached to it. All those hobbies above and more should be considered. He wants to speak into the framing of your shot, the lighting, the colors, the tone. Do you know why? Because he is the Creator of creativity. He is the standard of excellence, and every living thing reflects his beauty because he created it. He cares about helping you articulate and capture the best possible piece of art or creativity imaginable. He wants to be involved in the ideation, execution, and presentation of it.

So how do we practically do that? Well, over the years, I've put together four steps that have been beneficial for our ministry and creative partnerships. We've put this to use on all sorts of creative projects including events, movies, music, art, and more. This isn't a formula; the Lord isn't a math equation that needs to be solved. These are steps that encourage us to create space for him and help us invite him to be our creative partner. As you're going through these steps, note that these are best applied in the ideation and brainstorming phase of your creativity, and we will address further on what it looks like to continue to check in with him as you're actively creating. Let's jump in.

Begin to read over these and allow the Lord to stir something new. As usual, a prayer and meditation section at the end of the chapter will allow you to put this into practice.

Step 1: Prepare Your Heart

As we enter this prayer session with the Lord, we need to check our hearts. There is no room for ego in this space. Humble yourself before the Lord. Begin to lift his name up and thank him for his willingness to partner with you. Give thanks for everything you are about to receive. While you're doing this, take a look inward at yourself and make sure there is nothing unholy you are bringing into this partnership. Ask him if there is anything holding you back from dreaming with him. Repent of anything that seems to be lingering on your heart that doesn't belong. Remember, there is no room for our flesh here. Rebuke the enemy and any schemes that may attempt to sabotage this special time.

Step 2: Surrender

Begin to surrender your own visions and dreams. We may come into this prayer time with desires and even a direction we'd like it to go, but we need to fully give it to God. You need to release it all, fully; this is so pivotal. Remember the cookie dough. For this project to flourish, you need to trust him completely and remove anything that will hinder the process. Proverbs 3:5 says, "Trust in Yahweh with all your heart, and don't lean on your own understanding." This isn't the time for a partial surrender; write it all out and tell the Lord that you want his ways over yours.

Step 3: Listen

You've cleared your mind and heart. Now, it's time to be still. It can feel awkward at first, but this step is imperative. Close your eyes and listen, just as we talked about in the first chapter. We spend so much of our time talking; it's time to let him speak. You may have a song that comes to mind, you may see a specific color, or you may receive a word; that is between you and the Holy Spirit. Be okay sitting in the silence, and continue to wait for as long as you feel is necessary. Everyone hears from the Lord differently. Don't place him in a box and expect a certain result. Write down everything you see, hear, and feel; this is so important. Don't be discouraged if you don't get everything all at once, sometimes this takes multiple prayer sessions.

Step 4: Act

As your prayer time comes to a close, look through the various items you've written down and take them seriously. If you feel like there are some action steps needed, don't hesitate to pursue them. Passivity is real, and we often get hit with it right out of the gate. Sometimes an idea may seem bold or even absurd. If that's the case, spend more time praying about it, or even bring it to a fellow believer and ask them to pray with you. Remember, you're not alone in this journey, and obedience is key.

And there you have it. This book is over. Just kidding, where do we go from here and how do we apply this? Well, let me give you some advice that helps me and my team. As I mentioned above, this process should start in the ideation phase of your creativity. I absolutely love getting a team of folks together and going through this. We spend the first part of our time preparing our hearts and surrendering anything that would hinder us in this partnership, then corporately, yet individually, we seek his will for whatever we are praying about. We sit in silence, then after a set amount of time, we go around the room and share what we feel like the Lord said. Folks, let me tell you, there is something so special about seeing how the Spirit speaks to everyone in a unique way; it forms a sort of mosaic. You will notice how beautifully these things can come together when you seek his face as a creative team.

Boldness is necessary in the response time. Early on, I was with a rather large ministry team praying about an event that was being hosted in our town. During that prayer time, I felt like I saw a hot air balloon, but I was so quick to dismiss it. I thought that something like that was outlandish and would sound foolish for an event of this type. As we went around the room and shared what each of us heard in this quiet time, I remained quiet, sitting in my doubts. The next moment, someone next to me spoke up and mentioned that they heard something about a hot air balloon in their prayer time, then another person spoke up

① "YOUR WORD IS A ② LAMP to MY FEET ③ A LIGHT TO MY PATH

PSALMS · 119 : 105

and said they heard something similar. I'm sure you can imagine how I felt in that moment; it's something that I look back on and use as a learning experience. Be attentive in listening and be bold to share what you've heard.

This concept of co-creating with the Father isn't just limited to pre-production. He wants to be involved in the implementation of the art as well as the exhibition. We need to constantly remind ourselves to check in with the Lord during every step of our project. When I'm working with film teams, I will point out that everything from dialogue to camera framing, set design to audio placement, should be offered to the Lord. God is in the details, and he genuinely cares. We have to get ourselves to the point where we recognize God is the producer of these projects. His opinion and inspiration will go unmatched.

Let's sit here for a second on this. Are we treating God as just a voice of wisdom, or are we allowing him to influence every aspect of the project? We have the opportunity and invitation to come alongside the Creator of the universe, the One who gave us these dreams and visions in the first place. How much more do you think he cares about them than we do? He placed the talents in us for a reason; why would we ever try to do it alone? The answer is that we shouldn't.

Can you imagine a world in which Christian creatives as a whole began to fully rely on the Holy Spirit for ideas, inspiration, creating, editing, and displaying art? There would be an unstoppable new wave of excellence. I know there are so many anointed artists that are already doing this very thing, but we are approaching a movement and an awakening that will see an increased number of creatives leading the charge toward his kingdom. This isn't just limited to the Christian projects; God wants to be invited into all of them.

Remember that Western film I was working on a few years ago? The one where an actor and crew member asked me about hearing the voice of God? Well, that was just one of several stories. During my time on that set, spiritual conversations started happening regularly. I would have crew approach me and ask for prayer. Mind you, there happened to be a handful of Christians on this project, but the content wasn't explicitly faith-based. Well, one day, one of our leads, Chris, ended up getting hurt on set, and he experienced Jesus in a unique way. Chris wrote about it, and I want to share it with you:

> During an intense scene on my first day of shooting I rolled my ankle really bad. It was at the very least a bad sprain, and as time went on, I thought it was perhaps even fractured. The swelling was so severe I could hardly slip off my boot, and as the hours ticked by I couldn't put any weight on my ankle without intense shooting pain. A production assistant brought me a pair of crutches, and there I was, hobbling around location on crutches with a real concern that I might not be able to finish out the week.
>
> Before I went home for the night, one of our producers, Tyler Childs, asked if he could pray for me. Immediately our head of wardrobe asked to pray too, then the mother of one of our

actors, then our makeup artist, then a PA… so
I hobbled over to a folding chair, next to racks
of Old West costumes, hats, boots, gun belts…
and these people began to lay hands on me and
pray for healing. In the wardrobe room. On a
movie set. Surreal!

What happened next still gives me goosebumps.
It's hard to describe the sensation, but as they
were all praying, I suddenly felt a warmth in the
joint of my ankle. I remember thinking, "What
was that?!" Prayer ends and I stand up. No pain.
I put full weight on the injured ankle. No pain.
I take five or six steps forward. No pain. The
pain level had gone from a nine out of ten to
zero. I look up at the smiling faces of these crew
members and my jaw drops. "Are you kidding
me right now?!" I exclaimed. "That's God," one
of them said back to me.

I ended up walking back to my car that night
under my own power, leaving the crutches
propped up against the wall in that wardrobe
room, never to use them again. And I finished
the movie. This story is 100 percent true and I
still don't know what to make of it, other than
to say that God is very real, and he hears, and
he heals. I'm one of the most naturally skepti-
cal people I know, and even though my belief

system has always allowed for the "possibility" of God healing instantly, I had never experienced it firsthand until then. It was always
theological instead of experiential. Until that
moment.

Isn't God amazing? He healed Chris on our movie set and
displayed his glory in front of so many others that had never
witnessed God's supernatural power. I love sharing this story
over and over again because we can't limit the Father. His love
doesn't just operate in the faith-based entertainment world. I
am so honored to continue to see and hear stories like this one
happen across the globe. Continue to invite the Lord into every
aspect of your project and watch what happens.

Friends, I hope this new idea of co-creating with the Holy
Spirit gives you a lot to think about and a new perspective on
creativity moving forward. I pray that you will begin to create
space and opportunities to invite the Lord into your dreams
and visions. He is waiting for your invitation. What are you
waiting for?

REFLECT AND MEDITATE

Today's reflection and prayer will look different. We are going to put into practice what it means to partner with the Holy Spirit in creativity. I've written down the steps for you below. Spend some time praying and listening, and don't forget to write everything down!

Step 1: Prepare your Heart

- Check your heart.

- Humble yourself.

- Lift up the name of the Lord.

- Thank him for who he is and everything you are about to receive.

- Is there anything holding you back from fully dreaming with him?

- Repent for anything that doesn't belong.

- Rebuke the enemy and your flesh.

  Psalm 51:10: "Create in me a clean heart, O God. Renew a right spirit within me."

  Romans 12:2: "Don't be conformed to this world, but be transformed by the renewing of your mind, so that you may prove what is the good, well-pleasing, and perfect will of God."

Step 2: Surrender

- Surrender your own visions and dreams.

- Die to your flesh.

- Release it all to him.

- Place your trust in his hands.

- Remove anything that will hinder the process.

- Say out loud: "Lord, I surrender this project/dream/vision to you fully."

   Proverbs 3:5: "Trust in Yahweh with all your heart, and don't lean on your own understanding." This isn't the time for a partial surrender; write it all out and tell the Lord that you want his ways over yours.

   James 4:7: "Be subject therefore to God. Resist the devil, and he will flee from you."

Step 3: Listen

- Close your eyes and listen.

- Be still.

- Give him space.

- Write out everything you hear, see, and feel.

- Sit in the silence as long as you need to.

- The response may be different than you expected.

  Psalm 46:10: "Be still, and know that I am God. I will be exalted among the nations. I will be exalted in the earth."

  Psalm 119:105: "Your word is a lamp to my feet, and a light for my path."

Step 4: Act

- Take some time to go through your notes.

- Pray about what they might mean.

- Test them according to Scripture.

  2 Timothy 3:16-17: "Every Scripture is God-breathed and profitable for teaching, for reproof, for correction, and for instruction in righteousness, that each person who belongs to God may be complete, thoroughly equipped for every good work."

- Don't be passive in your action.

- The idea may be bold, but obedience is key.

Prayer

Lord, thank you for fresh vision and partnership with you. I ask that you give me peace as I move forward in this new order of operations with you. Help me to constantly surrender this to you and learn to follow your Spirit. I love you, Lord, and I trust you in this journey. Thank you for all you are doing in my life and creativity. Amen.

Use this space to write, sketch and respond to the Lord.

8

THE BALANCE

Let's take a look at Genesis 2:2-3: "On the seventh day God finished his work which he had done; and he rested on the seventh day from all his work which he had done. God blessed the seventh day, and made it holy, because he rested in it from all his work of creation which he had done."

We've spent time talking about creative excellence and all the attributes that make it up. Yet the concepts of rest and balance can often get left out. If I spent the whole book motivating you to create without telling you to rest, I would be setting you up for failure; it is easily overlooked in the creative world.

Artists tend to pour their hearts and souls into their projects, often at the cost of their own health and family. I know these are broad terms, but I've been there so many times and am grateful for a wife that constantly encourages me to find the balance.

Let's look at the verse above again. It says that the Lord rested "from all of his work of creation." The Lord clearly models the way for us in this passage. If the Creator of the universe took time to rest, don't you think you, in your finite flesh, should rest? Think about the things we start to give up when we forget to stop and rest. As a husband and father of three, my family and my relationship with Christ are usually the first things that get neglected. Then I start noticing a decline in my health followed by a drop in productivity. We weren't created to create nonstop; the Lord declared Sabbath and made it holy.

What is Sabbath, and why is it so important? Well, Sabbath—also known as *Shabbat* in Hebrew—literally means to "cease work." As if mentioning it in Genesis wasn't enough, we also see its importance later in Scripture. The Lord specifically made it law when he spoke to Moses on Mount Sinai. It's literally the fourth commandment.

Exodus 20:8-11 says, "Remember the Sabbath day, to keep it holy. You shall labor six days, and do all your work, but the seventh day is a Sabbath to Yahweh your God. You shall not do any work in it, you, nor your son, nor your daughter, your male servant, nor your female servant, nor your livestock, nor your stranger who is within your gates; for in six days Yahweh made heaven and earth, the sea, and all that is in them, and rested the seventh day; therefore Yahweh blessed the Sabbath day, and made it holy."

Imagine an Olympian trying to run without fuel. Sometimes, I have to visualize an empty well just to force myself to refuel and rest. We keep lowering the bucket, pulling water out until there is nothing left. Do we want to settle for an empty well or pursue a cup that runs over? I would prefer to create from an abundance of water of life rather than from a few drops at the bottom of a nearly empty well.

What does this look like? How do we rest and find a better balance in our lives? Honestly, the first thing that comes to my mind is sleep. There are so many benefits to a good night's sleep. Your health will improve, you'll come back to your project with fresh vision, and your body will thank you. Next, take time to just be present wherever you are. We live in a day and age where, even when we are clocked out, we are inundated with social media hype. Speaking from personal experience, I can sit and scroll for hours, but it comes at a cost. There are weeks when I've worked sixteen hours a day on a film set, but when I'm finally home for a day or two, it's easy to get glued to my phone.

Practice setting your phone down and getting out in nature. There is so much peace found in the Lord's creation. You may find new inspiration or fresh ideas while on a walk. Pick your ideal setting and get there, whether it's the mountains, the city, a beach, or anywhere else. Find the Lord in those moments and ask him for renewal.

Community is another place where we can find rest. Get together with friends and family. Allow others to pour into you. If you are extraverted, find a gathering or host one. If you are introverted, and the idea of feeling refreshed with a group sounds foreign, find a friend and get some one-on-one time. Creating can sometimes isolate us too much from the outside world; we need to just be with people to feel rejuvenated.

Consume entertainment. This may sound simple, but it's fun and worth it. Allow yourself to be entertained; watch a movie or a TV show. There is always inspiration to be found in story-telling. Focus on disengaging that creative side for a moment and enjoying someone else's art. Go to an art museum or watch

COME TO ME, All YOU
WHO labor AND ARE
HEAVY laden, I will
GIVE YOU REST

MATTHEW 11:28

a sports game; celebrate others who are thriving in their gifts. Give yourself a break from using your talents; you deserve it.

One of the most important things to do in this period of rest is seek the Lord's face. Just rest in his presence and allow him to speak life over you. During some of my quiet times, I literally lie there, soaking in worship. After you've partnered with him in creativity, rest with him. Spend time reading through the Word of God. It's really easy to be distracted in these moments with anxiety or your to-do lists, but set them aside and just sit with the Lord.

A common misconception is that taking time for rest will take away from your productivity and hinder progress on your projects. However, the truth is that prioritizing rest can actually increase your creativity for the project at hand. By taking care of your spiritual, physical, and emotional needs, you can approach your work with renewed energy and perspective. How do we truly sit back and allow ourselves to be present in our rest?

I want you to read several verses in Matthew. These verses have become a lifestyle for me and my family. Whenever I get stressed about the next project, the finances, or even just how to accomplish the task at hand, I take a moment and read this section of Matthew. I know this is a good chunk of Scripture but I want you to read every word and let the Lord speak over you.

Matthew 6:25-34 says:

> Therefore I tell you, don't be anxious for your life: what you will eat, or what you will drink; nor yet for your body, what you will wear. Isn't life more than food, and the body more than

clothing? See the birds of the sky, that they don't sow, neither do they reap, nor gather into barns. Your heavenly Father feeds them. Aren't you of much more value than they?

Which of you by being anxious, can add one moment to his lifespan? Why are you anxious about clothing? Consider the lilies of the field, how they grow. They don't toil, neither do they spin, yet I tell you that even Solomon in all his glory was not dressed like one of these. But if God so clothes the grass of the field, which today exists and tomorrow is thrown into the oven, won't he much more clothe you, you of little faith?

Therefore don't be anxious, saying, "What will we eat?", "What will we drink?" or, "With what will we be clothed?" For the Gentiles seek after all these things; for your heavenly Father knows that you need all these things. But seek first God's Kingdom and his righteousness; and all these things will be given to you as well. Therefore don't be anxious for tomorrow, for tomorrow will be anxious for itself. Each day's own evil is sufficient.

The Lord cares about you and your work, so much so that he wants you to focus on today, not tomorrow or yesterday. So what does the Lord have for you at this moment? I mentioned it earlier: be present, wherever you are. Be present when it's time to create, and be present when it's time to take a break.

Alright, now like a youth pastor preaching on relationships, let's talk about boundaries. We've explored what our weekends can look like, but for those of us that create for a career, are we clocking out when we need to? There comes a point at which our creativity becomes self-destructive. I get that there are deadlines and rhythms that force you to continue, but there is a line that we can often cross. Create boundaries with yourself and the creatives around you. Are you overworking yourself and not allowing yourself to take a break?

Guys, I've been blessed to partner with many different ministry creative teams all over the world, but there happens to be a common struggle. Each team is constantly overworking, and it's become accepted as normal. We can confuse working without ceasing with working in excellence for the Lord. They are two very different things. I've seen this expectation hung over creative teams' heads, and it's something that really bothers me. There are leaders that will convince a team that unrealistic deadlines and overnight edits are all for the Lord's glory. Don't get me wrong; there is a time and place to give something one final push, but we can't normalize burnout during holiday seasons in our ministries. This is coming from a place of personal experience.

So how do we fix that? Start planning ahead and be on purpose with pre-production. Factor in rest and give yourself a reasonable timeline. There are very few reasons to be creative in a time crunch. I know there is always the potential that people you work for and with may hinder the pre-production process. Be upfront about what it will cost you and your team. If you're a leader of a department, stand up for your team and fight for their family time and their rest time. Don't be aggressive and turn down every last-minute project that comes your way, but pray and ask if it's reasonable. Communicate both upstream and downstream. I am so grateful that I have had some leaders that were willing to tell their bosses exactly what their vision would cost us physically, emotionally, and spiritually. I know this is most often applied in church or ministry settings, but use it within any type of organization. Know your value and worth.

If the Lord has called you to work in the creative world, that isn't something that should be taken lightly. There will always be folks that look at our trade as one that doesn't provide a tangible output. They will argue that the face value of a project doesn't reflect the cost. They don't see the countless hours you've put in to get to this moment… the blood, sweat, and tears that have led to this very piece. The Lord sees you and knows how you've gotten to this point. Don't forget to pace yourself; we can feel lost without a healthy balance.

If you're looking for a sign to take a step back for a minute and breathe, this is it. Your art can wait; it doesn't have feelings that will get hurt. I think about the fruit I've seen from stepping away for a moment and the conversations I would have missed if I hadn't looked up. Keep up the good fight, friend; create your boundaries and learn to rest!

REFLECT AND MEDITATE

I encourage you to get alone and seek the Lord's face. Think about everything you've read in this chapter. What is the Lord speaking to you? I've written some questions below and provided two Bible verses to help guide your quiet reflection with the Lord.

Reflect

Am I taking time to rest?

What should a healthy creative balance look like?

What are ways I can rest?

Is my art draining me or filling me up?

Meditate

Matthew 11:28-30: "Come to me, all you who labor and are heavily burdened, and I will give you rest. Take my yoke upon you and learn from me, for I am gentle and humble in heart; and you will find rest for your souls. For my yoke is easy, and my burden is light."

Hebrews 4:9-11: "There remains therefore a Sabbath rest for the people of God. For he who has entered into his rest has himself also rested from his works, as God did from his. Let's therefore give diligence to enter into that rest, lest anyone fall after the same example of disobedience."

Prayer

Lord, thank you for your constant reminders to rest. I apologize for not always honoring Sabbath; help me to take a break and rest with you. Teach me what it truly means to balance my creative time. I choose to honor you in my creating and in my rest. Thank you for your inspiration and vision for my life. I love you, Lord, and seek to serve you with my gifts. Amen.

Use this space to write, sketch and respond to the Lord.

9

TL;DR

So there you have it. I've put everything out there for the taking. By no means am I an expert at any of this. In fact, this book has been speaking to me every day that I sit down and begin to write. I hope and pray that I've been able to help you wake up that inner creative and bring it into the fullness that the Lord so desperately desires the world to see. You have a gift, and it's time to begin using it in partnership with the Lord. With that being said, let's walk through and reflect on everything we've learned. You could call this the TL;DR chapter, meaning if you skimmed the whole book and landed here, you should be able to walk away with at least something valuable.

In the beginning of the book, we established that the Lord speaks to us. Clearly, he speaks to different people in different ways, so we don't need to compare our quiet time notes with our friends' notes. But I want you to think about the Jiminy Cricket quote from *Pinocchio*: "The still, small voice... Lord High Keeper of the knowledge of right and wrong, counselor in moments of temptation, and guide along the straight and narrow path." Write this down, put it on your wall, and remember it. The Holy Spirit is there to be with you, be your counselor in life, and guide you daily. Have you given him authority to do so? Continue to practice hearing his voice. Remember to wake up in the morning, greet the Lord, and then listen. He wants to speak to you.

The deeper we go with the Lord, the more we begin to find our identity in him instead of other things. Allow him to speak into you. As he does this, begin to ask him what is holding you back from pursuing him and the creativity he has set out for you. You were born to be creative. He placed dreams and visions on your heart for a reason; nothing is there by accident. Sometimes we allow wounds and doubt to hinder our pursuit. Is there anything holding you back from running toward the fullness the Lord is offering you?

Aside from ourselves, there will always be naysayers in our lives. Once I made an honest mistake on a project. When I asked how I could have handled it better, I was advised to walk away from the film world. I was fairly new to the film industry at the time, and I vividly remember having an anxiety attack on the project. Every part of me tried to quit filmmaking. I began looking for other careers and allowed fear to control me. My wife was amazing through the whole process and continued to encourage me to not give up. She reminded me that I was called to make movies, regardless of what other people thought. Despite her comments, I continued to avoid opportunities that would put me back on set.

One weekend, we ended up sitting in the front row of our church. Our pastor was preaching about pursuing our callings.

At one point, he said, "If the Lord has called you to something, don't give up. Why would you throw in the towel if you know that you are called?" That phrase hit me right in the bull's-eye. I began to tear up during the service; my wife nudged me every time he said to not give up. Later that same day, I received an opportunity to apply for a film role. As I read through the description of the position, I saw that it was everything I was trained to do, yet I heard the lies reverberating through my head. It's like the old cartoon visual: I had an angel on one shoulder and the devil on the other. One encouraged me to apply and get back into the game, while the enemy told me that I was worthless and would only fail again. My hands trembled as I filled out the application, and my heart raced when I finally hit send. Sure enough, I got the job and I truly believe it set me on course for where I am today. Shortly after that, I booked a job with National Geographic and the rest is history.

I can't imagine where I would be now if I had given up with a few negative words. There are so many people I look up to who experienced failure early on in their careers but persevered to become something more. How did they become great? Well, first they failed, moved past it, then figured out how to take their skill sets to the next level. That's what sets professional athletes and artists apart from the rest; they not only master something but execute it excellently.

We talked about artists throughout the ages who have excelled in their crafts and entertained the masses. *Entertainment* is one of the key words we can easily forget when we pursue creativity. I understand that the Lord may have placed a message in your heart, but if it's not entertaining and well-crafted, your audience will have a hard time connecting with it. We must continue to lead with a good story and allow our morals to shape it, instead of the other way around. Your art will always have meaning and can foster good conversations, but great artists learn how to marry a good story with a powerful message.

There are modern-day Christian artists who are leading the charge in the pursuit of creative excellence. Productions like *The Chosen* and *Jesus Revolution* are making waves in the creative community. They are actively choosing to tell good stories that have meaning and will impact people's lives. Not only are they choosing to make industry-standard projects, they are constantly looking at ways to bring more truth to the screen rather than just serve something palatable. I will continue to celebrate with these artists and the people that get behind them. They are a part of a creative awakening that is happening within the body of Christ.

Filmmakers, storytellers, musicians, and all artists alike are feeling a call to something larger than themselves. We choose to find our identity in Christ rather than our art. When we do that, we are no longer forced to place our art in a box. Our art will be shaped by our identity in the Lord, and we will naturally reflect his glory when we use our gifts to create. Sometimes we are called to create pieces that are used for evangelism, and sometimes we are called to make pieces purely for entertainment. There are more and more artists that are going into Hollywood as Christians and actively living out Colossians 3:23, which says, "And whatever you do, work heartily, as for the Lord, and not for men." They are becoming the best sound guys, actors, and writers—not for men but for the Lord.

ARISE,

SHINE FOR YOUR lIGHT
HAS COME, AND THE
GLORY of THE LORD RISES
UPON   YOU
ISAIAH 60:1

Let's sit here for a second. When we work diligently for the Lord in anything and everything, it glorifies God. Think about how much our surroundings can be affected by that type of pursuit. When we aim to do our best—not for man but for God—it creates a different kind of impact. Being a light on set doesn't necessarily mean sharing the gospel to everyone around you. Sometimes it can mean just holding your moral ground when others are making poor decisions. Or sometimes it means respecting others as you'd want to be respected. You'd be surprised how far a little respect goes in the film world. Remember to stand on what you believe in; don't compromise on your beliefs. You don't always have to tell everyone you're a Christian, just allow Christ to work through you.

On the other hand, you may have times where the Lord leads you to use your words in addition to your actions. Make sure you're obedient in those moments. I remember the first time I felt the Lord ask me to step out in boldness and offer prayer to an individual on a secular set. It was scary, and I felt so vulnerable while I did it, but I was humbled by the response. You'd be surprised how many people are open to receiving a prayer of blessing. Don't force it; walk in the Spirit, and move as he guides you.

We talked about inviting the Lord into every aspect of our art. It starts with creating space for the Lord and allowing him to speak into every situation as an active creative partner. Remember to prepare your heart, submit everything to him, listen for his response, and then act in obedience to his direction. You've got to get yourself out of the way and allow the Lord to work fully on your project. Enter into each prayer with an honest, repentant heart, and give thanks for everything God has done and will do.

As you move into the submission step, begin to release your own ideas and visions. Remember the cookie dough story; don't let your flesh hinder the process. Proverbs 3:6 says, "In all your ways acknowledge him, and he will make your paths straight." Once you've laid it all out on the table, give the Lord space to speak. Open your ears, open your spirit, and write everything down. Don't walk away from your prayer time until you feel that he's said all he needs to in that moment. He will begin to help you shape your project during each phase of production. He doesn't just want to help you with the heading; continue to invite him into the creation, the polishing, and the presentation. He's the Creator of creativity, so he has the best ideas!

Take the Lord's direction and run with everything you've got toward the visions set out before you. Continue to grow in your skills and constantly be looking for new ways to approach your art. Challenge yourself to get better and make better art. This pursuit of excellence will feel different, but you have the Lord as the wind in your sails. Find a community that will help pour into you and make sure you are always rooted in the Word of God.

But don't forget about the balance. Take time to rest and evaluate each step of the process. Sometimes rest can be viewed as a distraction or something that would take away your productivity... It's definitely not. Step back when you need to get a healthy perspective. It's easy to keep our heads down and get lost in our art, but we must remember to come up for air. Go on walks, spend time with family and friends, and allow yourself to recharge. Sabbath is a commandment and is beneficial not only to your art but to your personal well-being. Take care of yourself and make sure you're working hard for the right reasons.

Comparison and insecurity aren't from the Lord. You have nothing to prove to anyone. He sees you and loves you; focus on who he has called you to be.

Friend, I believe in you! You picked this book up for a reason. Hopefully by now, you've got something burning deep inside, ready to be birthed into fruition. If you don't, no worries; ask the Lord where you're supposed to go now. I am so honored to be able to share these stories and lessons I've learned with you. If there is something in this book that challenged you or inspired you, please reach out. I'd love to hear from you. It has been such an honor to write this book and simply be a vessel for the Holy Spirit. Hopefully this is the first of many, so thank you for coming along on this journey. This is the part where I will say goodbye, but not without one final blessing for you. Please take a minute to read it, allow the Lord to speak over you and then spend some time responding. Blessings my friends!

Change the World

Sons and daughters, the time is now. Go forth and pursue the dreams the Lord has set out before you. You must not hesitate to run at them any longer. Ask the Lord for courage, and you will find it. There is a shift coming, and you are called to be a part of it. Step out of the shadows and into the fullness that the Father has prepared for you. Shrug off anything that hinders the pursuit of your calling. There is fresh vision for those who seek his face. The Lord stands, awaiting your invitation.

Rise up and feel the wind in your sails; a new momentum is building. Don't fight it; allow it to shape you, guide you, and push you to become who you were destined to be. New wine is coming, but do not forget that you first must present a new wineskin to receive it. The Lord is looking to sharpen your character and grow you into the dreamer you are destined to be. Seek wise counsel and surround yourself with like-minded individuals.

The time is now: Awaken O Dreamer!

REFLECT AND MEDITATE

*I encourage you to get alone and seek the Lord's face.
Think about everything you've read in this book.*

Reflect

Lord, what dreams would you have me pursue?

How do you want me to accomplish them?

What do you need me to learn in the process?

What are my next steps?

Meditate

*Isaiah 60:1: "Arise, shine; for your light has come, and
Yahweh's glory has risen on you!"*

Use this space to write, sketch and respond to the Lord.

About the Author

Tyler W. Childs is an experienced film and TV producer with a portfolio of projects that have taken him to over 15 countries. He has collaborated with major networks such as National Geographic Wild and coordinated films with well known talent from Disney, Marvel, DC and more. In addition to filmmaking, Tyler is passionate about storytelling and teaches ministries through his non-profit organization, Parable International. By combining his love of filmmaking with his desire to make a difference, Tyler has helped to inspire a new generation of storytellers. Along with his wife (Becca) and three children (Riverlyn, Zion & Eden), Tyler has spent the last 2 years traveling full-time in an RV while producing movies and working with ministries.

If you would like to get in touch with Tyler or his team, you may do so through Parable International's website, they'd love to hear from you!

www.parableint.org